ENJOY!

MORE RECIPES FROM THE BEST OF BRIDGE

SECOND EFFORT
"TWENTY-SEVENTH TIME 'ROUND"

WRITTEN AND PUBLISHED BY:

THE BEST OF BRIDGE PUBLISHING LTD.

6037-6ᵀᴴ STREET S.E.

CALGARY, ALBERTA. T2H 1C8.

PRINTED IN CANADA BY CENTAX BOOKS

A DIVISION OF PRINTWEST COMMUNICATIONS LTD.

HAND LETTERED BY NORM W. HODGINS

PHOTOGRAPHY BY COMMERCIAL ILLUSTRATORS LTD.

COPYRIGHT © 1980 BY BEST OF BRIDGE PUBLISHING LTD.

ISBN- 09690425-1-5

No Laughing!

THE LADIES OF THE BRIDGE ARE WARM INSIDE WHEN WE STOP OUR JOKING LONG ENOUGH TO CONSIDER THIS PAGE AND WHAT TO INCLUDE. THE TREMENDOUS SUPPORT WE HAVE RECEIVED FROM EVERY ANGLE, THAT HAS MADE SOMETHING MAGIC HAPPEN TO AN IDEA AND TO US AS WOMEN — FROM OUR RETAILERS WHOM WE REGARD AS FRIENDS; OUR MAIL ORDER CROWD WHO KEEP US COMPANY WHEN IT'S BUSINESS AS USUAL; THE MEDIA WHO HAVE GIVEN US TIME AND CONSIDERATION; THE WOMEN WHO HAVE VOLUNTEERED THEIR FAVORITES AND ENDURED OUR ENDLESS DIALOGUE; AND ALL THE MEN WHO HAVE LAUGHED AT OUR JOKES AND STARTED TO COOK; WE THANK YOU FOREVER —

KAREN BRIMACOMBE   HELEN MILES

LINDA JACOBSON   VAL ROBINSON

MARY KORMAN   JOAN WILSON

MARILYN LYLE

CANADIAN CATALOGUING IN PUBLICATION DATA
MAIN ENTRY UNDER TITLE:
ENJOY! MORE RECIPES FROM THE BEST OF BRIDGE

INCLUDES INDEX.
ISBN 0-9690425-1-5

1. LUNCHEONS. 2. SUPPERS. 3. DESSERTS.
I. TITLE: BEST OF BRIDGE.
TX715. E55 1979 641.5'3 C80-9003-9

PRINTED IN CANADA

FOREWARMING

WE HAVE NOW TRAVELLED ALL OVER MAINLAND CANADA, RAVING ABOUT OURSELVES AND OUR "BEST". PEOPLE WHO HAVE SEEN US ON PROMOTIONAL TRIPS WILL COME UP, POINT AND SAY "SO THAT'S WHAT THEY LOOK LIKE!" - AND THEN LAUGH. SURELY THEY'RE LAUGHING AT THEIR FAVORITE ONE LINER FONDLY REMEMBERED, NOT AT US DIRECTLY. WE HAVE NOW SOLVED THE IMAGE PROBLEM OF PEOPLE THINKING OF US AS COOKING AUTHORITIES - DEMONSTRATING HAMBURGER SOUP IN DEPARTMENT STORE AISLES WITH A HUNK OF RAW MEAT CLINGING TO YOUR CHEEK IS NOT CONDUCIVE TO A PROFESSIONAL AURA.

AT HOME, LIFE IS WORSE. OUR CHILDREN TALK LIKE EITHER PROMOTERS, PUBLISHERS OR PAPER PUSHERS. OUR HUSBANDS, WHO ORIGINALLY THOUGHT THAT "THE BEST OF BRIDGE" WAS A CUTE IDEA THAT MIGHT KEEP THEIR LITTLE LADIES BUSY WHILE THEY WERE OUT FIGHTING MAD DOGS IN THE JUNGLE, ARE NOW WELL AWARE OF WHAT THE JUNGLE REALLY IS - THAT'S THE HOUSE WHEN THE CULINARY MAGNATE IS AWAY, WINING AND DINING ON YET ANOTHER PROMOTIONAL TOUR. THE FAMILY CAN'T UNDERSTAND WHY OUR OWN COOKING HASN'T IMPROVED. "MOM'S LASAGNE RECIPE

IS IN THE BOOK, BUT WHEN MAKING IT SHE <u>STILL</u> ALWAYS HAS A LAYER LEFTOVER." EVERYONE IS BIGGER, OURSELVES INCLUDED. NO BABIES ARE AMONG US, AND, THANK GOODNESS, THE KIDS STILL LIKE WIENERS AND BEANS. THINGS HAVE BEEN BETTER LATELY, AS WE'RE BACK TO TESTING ALL OUR RECIPES SO THAT WE CAN AVOID EXPRESSIONS SUCH AS "A WAD OF THIS" OR A "SQUIRT OF THAT." AFTER ONE WEEK OF NOTHING BUT CONTINUAL GASTRONOMICAL ADVENTURES, ONE OF THE BOYS REFUSED TO BE A GUINEA PIG ANY LONGER AND OPTED FOR A PEANUT BUTTER SANDWICH. OUR BIGGEST PROBLEM WAS PUSHING THE ELEPHANT THROUGH THE DOOR WHEN MAKING THAT SOUP, BUT IT WAS WELL WORTH THE EFFORT.

DID WE REALLY WELCOME ALL THE COMMENTS AND/OR CRITICISMS? YOU BET, AND DO WE GET LETTERS - <u>LOTS</u> OF LETTERS. THEY'RE ABSOLUTELY THE GREATEST. LONG ONES TELLING US ABOUT THEIR FAMILIES AND BRIDGE CLUBS (IT'S TERRIFIC TO KNOW THAT PEOPLE STILL PLAY!) AND SHORT ONES ASKING FOR A NEW 'SPINE' (THAT'S A COIL) FOR THEIR BOOK AS THEIR DOG JUST ATE THEIRS'. PEOPLE WRITE TO SAY WHERE THEY'VE SENT "THE

BEST OF BRIDGE" - ONE WENT TO THE ORIENT AND THE RECIPIENT NOW COOKS 'CANADIAN' ONCE A WEEK. ANOTHER EXPRESSED INTEREST IN BUYING SOME OF THE CHINA PICTURED. WE ALSO GET QUESTIONS - WHICH WE ENDEAVOUR TO ANSWER - OUR RECIPES ARE LIKE THE ONES YOU GET FROM A FRIEND, EXCEPT <u>WE</u> INCLUDE ALL THE INGREDIENTS. AND, OF COURSE, ALWAYS THE QUESTION: "WHEN ARE YOU GOING TO DO ANOTHER BOOK?"

WE DIDN'T LEAP INTO WRITING THIS SECOND EDITION BECAUSE WE WANTED TO MAKE IT BETTER - NOT JUST AS GOOD AS - THE FIRST. YOU CAN TELL OUR LIFESTYLES ARE CHANGING BY THE RECIPES WE'VE KEYED IN ON - MORE TIME TO MAKE APPETIZERS AS THERE AREN'T BABIES TO BURP AS THE GUESTS ARE POURING THROUGH THE DOOR ½ HOUR EARLY (OR WERE WE ALWAYS A ½ HOUR LATE?). THE LARGE SECTION ON VEGETABLES IS HEALTHY TOKENISM TO OFFSET THE CALORIC CONTENT OF DESSERTS IN THE LAST BOOK, AND THE MAIN COURSE CASSEROLES AND SOUPS ARE THERE BECAUSE THEY'RE MAKE - AHEADS, FREEZABLES AND SIMPLE WITH GOURMET RESULTS.

WE ASK YOU TO JOIN US - RELAX, LAUGH AND "ENJOY" OUR "BEST" - EVERYONE ELSE WILL TOO!

PICTURED ON COVER:

CASSEROLES

JAMBALAYA

PAGE 153

CRAB STUFFED CHICKEN BREASTS

PAGE 124

COQUILLE DAVID

PAGE 122

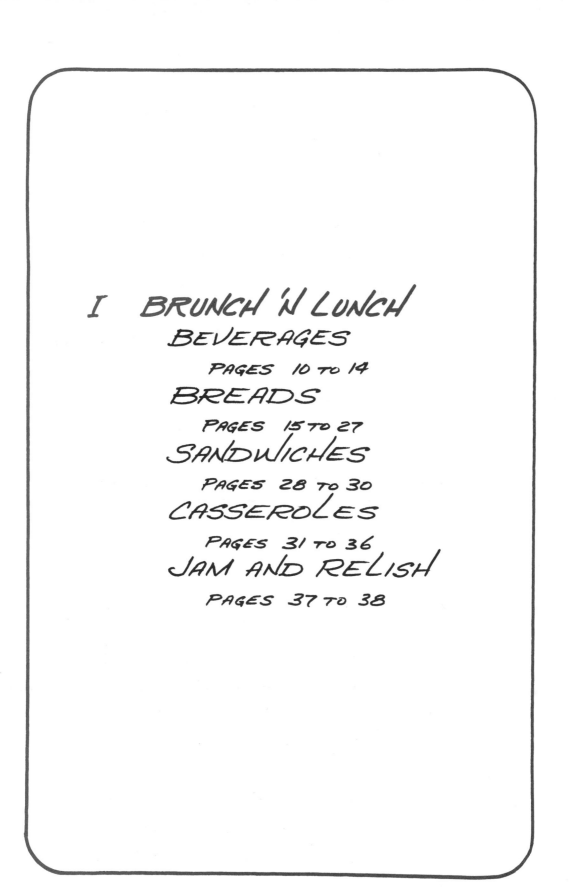

I BRUNCH 'N LUNCH

Hot Rum Canadienne

Marvelous after skiing, after football games, after tobogganing, after anything!

    2   oz. dark rum
    2   tbsps. maple syrup
        squirt of lemon juice
        nutmeg
        cinnamon (a cinnamon stick is best)
        boiling water
        dab of butter

Combine first five ingredients, top off with <u>boiling</u> water and a small dab of butter. Makes one steaming mug.

Dickery Daiquiri Docks

    1   6 1/4 oz. can frozen lemonade
    1   6 1/4 oz. can limeade
    1   6 1/4 oz. can unsweetened lemon juice
    3   cans white rum
    3   cans water

Mix all ingredients in plastic container. Place in freezer overnight. Remove 10 minutes before serving. Serves 8.

Mongolian Dingbats

- 1 oz. Vodka
- 1 oz. Kahlua
- 1 oz. Tia Maria Liqueur
- 4 oz. Cream
- Ice

Combine all ingredients in glass. These turn you into one. Do not light a match! One serving.

They call our language the mother tongue because father seldom gets a chance to use it.

Gerry's Morning Flip

- 6 Ice Cubes
- 1 6 1/4 oz. Can Frozen Lemonade
- 1 6 1/4 oz. Can Gin
- 2 6 1/4 oz. Cans Cold Water
- 2 drops Almond Flavouring
- 1 Egg
- 1 to 2 tbsps. Lemon Juice

Combine all ingredients in blender- blend well and serve in stem glasses. Serves 4.

BLENDER BREAKFAST

A FAST AND NUTRITIOUS BREAKFAST FOR THOSE WHO NEVER HAVE TIME.

1   EGG
1   TBSP. LIQUID HONEY
3/4 CUP APRICOT NECTAR
1/4 CUP PINEAPPLE JUICE

COMBINE ALL INGREDIENTS IN BLENDER AND WHIRL UNTIL SMOOTH. ONE SERVING.

A HOBBY IS GETTING EXHAUSTED ON YOUR OWN TIME.

SKIP AND GO NAKED

WHAT ELSE CAN YOU DO WHEN IT'S HOT?

1   6 1/4 oz. CAN FROZEN LEMONADE
1   6 1/4 oz. CAN WATER
1   6 1/4 oz. CAN GIN
4   ICE CUBES
1   BOTTLE BEER, COLD

PLACE LEMONADE, WATER, GIN AND ICE CUBES IN BLENDER. BLEND UNTIL ICE IS CRUSHED. POUR INTO 4 MEDIUM GLASSES AND TOP WITH BEER.

Winter Punch

Fun to serve the gals when they arrive for bridge on those cold winter nights. Serves 8.

6	cups apple juice
2	cups cranberry cocktail
1	tsp. bitters
4	oz. cinnamon red hots
1	cup rum (light)
2	cinnamon sticks
16	cloves

Tie cinnamon sticks and cloves in a cheese cloth bag. Mix rest of ingredients, except rum, together and place cheese cloth bag in mixture. Simmer in a large pot for 45 minutes. Add one cup rum or <u>more</u>. You may want to double this recipe because they'll want more.

Blueberry Tea

Some blueberries! One serving.

½	oz. Grand Marnier liqueur
½	oz. Amaretto liqueur
	tea, hot.

In a cup, place each of the liqueurs. Add tea. This is a super end to dinner!

Hello Sunshine!

Good Bye Brain!

    3   oz. sparkling white wine
    3   oz. orange juice
        ice - optional
Combine all ingredients and drink!
Makes one serving. (see Picture).

The Modern girl wears just as
many clothes as her Grandma, but
not all at the same time.

Coffee Brandy Freeze

A simply delicious way to end an
elegant meal. You deserve it!

    1   Litre Coffee Ice Cream
    ½   cup Brandy
        Shaved Chocolate (semi-sweet)
Set ice cream out while you clear
the table so it is soft. Combine ice
cream and brandy in a blender. Blend
until all lumps disappear. Serve in
your prettiest long stemmed glasses.
Shave chocolate on top and serve.
(I suggest you have extra ingredients on
hand). So simple and so...oo good. Serves 4 to 6

14

Super Blueberry Lemon Muffins

These will disappear as quickly as you make them!

2	cups flour
½	cup sugar
3	tsps. baking powder
½	tsp. salt
	rind of one lemon
1	egg
1	cup milk
½	cup butter, melted
1	cup fresh, frozen or canned blueberries

Topping

½	cup melted butter
1	tbsp. lemon juice
½	cup white sugar

Mix flour, sugar, baking powder, salt and lemon rind in large bowl. Beat egg in medium sized bowl, add milk and butter. Add egg mixture to dry ingredients. Stir until just mixed (batter will be lumpy). Stir in blueberries. Fill muffin pans 2/3 full and bake at 425° for 20 minutes.

For topping see page 16

Super Blueberry Lemon Muffins

Continued from Page 15

TOPPING - Combine melted butter and lemon juice. Measure sugar in separate dish. Take slightly cooled muffins and dunk top into butter and then sugar. Makes 16 large or 32 small muffins. (See Picture).

Orange Honey Bread

2	Tbsps. Shortening
1	Cup Honey
1	Egg, well beaten
1½	Tsps. Grated Orange Rind
2½	Cups Flour
2½	Tsps. Baking Powder
½	Tsp. Baking Soda
½	Tsp. Salt
¾	Cup Orange Juice
¾	Cup Chopped Nuts

Cream shortening and honey. Add egg and rind. Sift flour with baking powder, baking soda and salt. Add to honey mixture alternately with juice. Add nuts. Put in greased 9" x 5" loaf pan and bake 1 hour and 10 minutes at 325°.

16

PICTURED ON OVERLEAF:

HELLO SUNSHINE!
       PAGE 14
CHRISTMAS MORNING WIFESAVER
       PAGE 33
(JARS)
1. SOYA ALMONDS
       PAGE 55
2. CHRISTMAS MARMALADE
       PAGE 37
3. SPICED PECANS
       PAGE 57
(MUFFINS)
1. SUPER BLUEBERRY LEMON MUFFINS
       PAGE 15
2. APPLE CINNAMON MUFFINS
       PAGE 21
(CAKE)
CHRISTMAS COFFEE CAKE
       PAGE 23

COFFEE CAN BREAD

THIS IS A SIMPLE NO-YEAST BREAD.

2   TBSPS. HONEY OR SUGAR
3   CUPS FLOUR OR . . . .
>   1 CUP WHEAT GERM
>   1 CUP WHOLE WHEAT FLOUR
>   1 CUP OATMEAL

2   TSPS. BAKING POWDER
1/2   TSP. BAKING SODA
1/2   TSP. SALT
1 3/4   CUPS MILK

MIX DRY INGREDIENTS IN LARGE BOWL. STIR IN MILK AND HONEY. PUT IN A WELL GREASED 1 LB. COFFEE CAN AND COVER WITH FOIL. LET STAND 5 MINUTES. BAKE AT 350° FOR 1 1/2 HOURS. LET COOL 5 TO 10 MINUTES AND TURN OUT.

NOTE: IF YOU DON'T HAVE A COFFEE CAN, A LOAF PAN WILL DO - JUST REDUCE BAKING TIME BY ABOUT 20 MINUTES.

A SMART GIRL IS ONE WHO KNOWS HOW TO PLAY TENNIS, PIANO AND DUMB.

BLUEBERRY COFFEE CAKE

4 EGGS, SEPARATED
1¾ CUPS SUGAR
3 TSPS. VANILLA
1 CUP OIL
   JUICE AND RIND OF 2 LEMONS
2½ CUPS FLOUR
2 TSPS. BAKING POWDER
2 CUPS FROZEN BLUEBERRIES (FLOURED)

BEAT EGG WHITES UNTIL FROTHY, ADD SUGAR, EGG YOLKS, OIL, VANILLA, LEMON JUICE AND RIND. FOLD IN DRY INGREDIENTS AND FLOURED BLUEBERRIES, RESERVING A HANDFUL FOR THE BOTTOM OF THE PAN. PLACE RESERVED BLUEBERRIES IN BOTTOM OF 10" BUNDT OR TUBE PAN. POUR IN BATTER AND BAKE AT 350° FOR 1 HOUR. WHEN COOL, TURN OUT ON CAKE PLATE AND WAIT FOR THE RAVES!!

MAYBE HARD WORK WON'T KILL A MAN, BUT ON THE OTHER HAND, WHO EVER HEARD OF ANYONE RESTING TO DEATH?

GOOD OLD FASHIONED GINGER BREAD

THIS RECIPE HAS BEEN PASSED DOWN IN MY FAMILY FOR SEVERAL GENERATIONS. IT'S DELICIOUS SERVED WARM WITH A TOPPING OF WHIPPED CREAM, BUTTERED, OR WITH THE FOLLOWING FLUFFY LEMON CREAM.

¼	CUP SHORTENING OR BUTTER
¼	CUP WHITE SUGAR
½	CUP MOLASSES
½	TSP. BAKING SODA
1	TSP. EACH; CINNAMON, GINGER, CLOVES AND SALT.
¾	CUP BOILING WATER
1¼	CUPS FLOUR
1	TSP. BAKING POWDER
1	BEATEN EGG
¼	TSP. BAKING SODA

CREAM THE SUGAR AND BUTTER. SIFT CINNAMON, GINGER, CLOVES, SALT, BAKING POWDER AND FLOUR. BEAT ½ TSP. BAKING SODA INTO MOLASSES UNTIL FLUFFY. ADD TO SUGAR-BUTTER MIXTURE. ADD ¼ TSP. BAKING SODA TO THE BOILING WATER. ADD THIS ALTERNATELY WITH THE DRY INGREDIENTS TO THE MOLASSES MIXTURE. FOLD IN BEATEN EGG. POUR INTO GREASED LOAF PAN AND BAKE 30 MINUTES AT 400°. THE BATTER WILL BE THIN.

Good Old Fashioned Ginger Bread

FLUFFY LEMON CREAM TOPPING

8	oz. cream cheese, softened
½	cup sifted confectioners powdered sugar
¼	cup light cream
½	tsp. lemon extract

Blend cream cheese, sugar, cream and lemon extract together in a small bowl. Chill slightly and serve on warm ginger bread.

Pumpkin Loaf

3	cups flour
1	tsp. soda
1	tsp. salt
3	tsps. cinnamon
2	cups pumpkin, canned
2	cups white sugar
4	eggs
1¼	cups oil

Mix dry ingredients in bowl. Make a well in centre. Add the remaining ingredients and stir just enough to mix. Pour into two 9" x 5" loaf pans. Bake at 350° for 1 hour.

Apple Cinnamon Muffins

A pleasant change for your family breakfast or an after school treat! (See picture).

2	cups flour
1/2	cup white sugar
3	tsps. baking powder
1/2	tsp. cinnamon
1/2	tsp. salt
1/2	cup butter
1	large apple, peeled and diced
1/4	cup walnuts, finely chopped
1	egg
2/3	cup milk
1	tsp. cinnamon
1	tbsp. brown sugar

Sift flour, sugar, baking powder, 1/2 tsp. cinnamon and salt into large bowl. Cut in butter with pastry blender. Measure out 1/4 cup and reserve for topping. Add apple and nuts to flour mixture. Beat egg in a small bowl and add milk. Pour into flour mixture and stir until just mixed (batter will be lumpy). Spoon into lightly greased muffin pans - 2/3 full. Add 1 tsp. cinnamon and brown sugar to reserved topping mixture. Sprinkle over each muffin. Bake at 425° for 15 to 20 minutes. Makes 16 large or 32 small muffins.

LEMON LOAF

1	CUP SUGAR
½	CUP BUTTER
2	EGGS, BEATEN
½	CUP MILK
1½	CUPS FLOUR
1	TSP. BAKING POWDER
1	TSP. SALT
	RIND OF 1 LEMON, FINELY GRATED
½	CUP CHOPPED WALNUTS (OPTIONAL)

DRIZZLE

	JUICE OF 1 LEMON
¼	CUP SUGAR

CREAM BUTTER AND SUGAR. ADD BEATEN EGGS AND MILK. ADD DRY INGREDIENTS (NO SIFTING REQUIRED), LEMON RIND AND WALNUTS. MIX WELL. BAKE IN 9"x5" GREASED LOAF PAN FOR 1 HOUR AT 350°. REMOVE FROM OVEN AND COOL FOR 5 MINUTES. PRICK CRUST WITH FORK AND POUR DRIZZLE OVER LOAF. ALLOW TO STAND AT LEAST 1 HOUR BEFORE REMOVING FROM PAN.

WHAT CAN YOU EXPECT OF A DAY THAT STARTS WITH GETTING UP?

CHRISTMAS COFFEE CAKE

PRETTY AND DECORATIVE - MAKES A NICE
LITTLE GIFT. (SEE PICTURE).

    18 TO 20 PECAN HALVES
    12 TO 14 CHERRY HALVES
    1/3   CUP BUTTER
    1/3   CUP BROWN SUGAR
    1 1/2 CUPS FLOUR
    1 1/2 TSPS. BAKING POWDER
    1   TSP. BAKING SODA
    1   CUP BROWN SUGAR
    1/4   CUP BUTTER
    2   EGGS
    1   TSP. VANILLA
    1   CUP SOUR CREAM

MELT 1/3 CUP BUTTER. ADD 1/3 CUP BROWN
SUGAR AND STIR. PLACE IN THE BOTTOM OF
A 10" TUBE OR BUNDT PAN. DECORATE THE
BOTTOM WITH CHERRY AND PECAN HALVES.
CREAM 1/4 CUP BUTTER AND 1 CUP BROWN
SUGAR. ADD VANILLA AND EGGS. BEAT UNTIL
FLUFFY. BLEND IN SOUR CREAM. MIX FLOUR,
BAKING POWDER, BAKING SODA AND SIFT.
MAKE A WELL IN CENTRE OF DRY INGREDIENTS,
ADD LIQUIDS AND STIR GENTLY. POUR IN
GREASED PAN AND BAKE AT 350° FOR 30
MINUTES.

FERGOSA

(An Italian Bread)

This is a great accompaniment with salad for a ladies lunch or great with salmon or homemade soup. Everyone will love it — you'd better make two. (See picture).

½ cup chopped onion
1 tbsp. butter
1 cup tea bisk
½ cup grated cheddar cheese
⅓ cup milk
1 cup grated cheddar cheese
1 egg, slightly beaten
  poppy seeds

Sauté onion and butter until the onion is transparent. Meanwhile, combine the tea bisk, ½ cup grated cheese and milk and beat until smooth. This will be sticky. Knead 10 times on floured board working in small amount of flour if it's sticking too much. Butter 8" or 9" pie pan and also your hands. Spread this mixture on the bottom of the pan. Combine the cup of grated cheddar and egg. Spread on crust, sprinkle with onion-butter mixture and poppy seed. Bake at 425° for 20 minutes. To serve, cut in wedges. Serves 8.

Zucchini Loaves

- 3 EGGS
- 1 CUP OIL
- 2 CUPS SUGAR
- 1 TSP. VANILLA
- 2 CUPS WASHED, FINELY SHREDDED, UNPARED ZUCCHINI-WELL PACKED
- 1½ CUPS CAKE FLOUR
- 1 CUP WHOLE WHEAT FLOUR
- ½ CUP WHEAT GERM
- 1 TSP. SALT
- 2 TSPS. NUTMEG
- 1 TSP. BAKING SODA
- ½ TSP. BAKING POWDER
- ½ CUP CHOPPED NUTS

IN A BOWL BEAT EGGS, OIL, SUGAR, VANILLA AND ZUCCHINI. TURN BEATERS ON LOW AND BEGIN ADDING ALL REMAINING INGREDIENTS AS YOU MEASURE THEM. STIR IN NUTS LAST. BATTER IS QUITE THIN. LINE TWO 9" × 5" GLASS LOAF PANS WITH BUTTERED DOUBLE WAX PAPER. POUR ⅔ FULL AND BAKE 1 HOUR AT 325°.

THERE IS NO JUSTIFICATION FOR SPITTING IN ANOTHER MAN'S FACE, UNLESS HIS MUSTACHE IS ON FIRE.

L'il Red's Apricot Bread

Very moist. Excellent served with mild white cheese, and it freezes well.

1 cup chopped dried apricots
1 cup water
1 large orange- rind and juice
2 tbsps. shortening
1 cup white sugar
2 eggs, beaten
1 tsp. vanilla
2 cups flour
2 tsps. baking powder
1 tsp. baking soda
½ tsp. salt
½ cup raisins
1 cup chopped walnuts

Add water to apricots and let stand overnight. Drain liquid and reserve. Add orange juice to apricot liquid and enough water to make 1 cup in total. Cream shortening, grated orange rind and sugar. Add beaten eggs and vanilla. Sift dry ingredients and add alternately with the 1 cup of liquid. Mix in apricots, raisins and walnuts. Pour into 6" x 10" x 2½" greased loaf pan. Bake at 350° for 60 to 70 minutes.

SOUR CREAM COFFEE CAKE

6	TBSPS. SOFT BUTTER
1	CUP WHITE SUGAR
2	EGGS (ROOM TEMPERATURE)
1⅓	CUPS FLOUR
1½	TSPS. BAKING POWDER
1	TSP. BAKING SODA
1	TSP. CINNAMON
1	CUP SOUR CREAM
6	OZ. PKG. SEMI-SWEET CHOCOLATE CHIPS
1	TBSP. SUGAR

BEAT BUTTER, SUGAR AND EGGS IN BOWL FOR 10 MINUTES. SIFT DRY INGREDIENTS AND BLEND INTO SOUR CREAM. BLEND BOTH MIXTURES TOGETHER BY HAND. MIX WELL AND POUR BATTER INTO GREASED AND FLOURED 9" x 13" PAN. SCATTER CHOCOLATE CHIPS OVER TOP. SPRINKLE 1 TBSP. SUGAR OVER TOP. BAKE AT 350° FOR 35 MINUTES OR UNTIL DONE. COOL IN PAN ON WIRE RACK AND KEEP AT ROOM TEMPERATURE.

30 IS A NICE AGE FOR A WOMAN—
ESPECIALLY IF SHE HAPPENS TO BE 40.

SHRIMP SANDWICHES

These are always a hit and really filling. (Have you tried alfalfa sprouts on a peanut butter sandwich?).

2	slices, 7 grain bread, buttered
1/2	cup cooked frozen baby shrimp, thawed and rinsed
1/4	cup alfalfa sprouts
1/2	an avacado, sliced
	lemon juice
	mayonnaise

Place shrimp on one buttered bread slice. Top with sprouts and place avacado slices over all. Sprinkle liberally with fresh squeezed lemon juice. Spread mayonnaise on second slice of bread and place on top of avacado. Slice diagonally. Serves one.

They say hardwork never killed anyone, but why take a chance on being the first casualty.

Stuffed Ham Loaf

1	LOAF UNSLICED ITALIAN BREAD
1/4	CUP MAYONNAISE OR SALAD DRESSING
1/3	CUP CHOPPED PARSLEY
1	8 OZ. PKG. CREAM CHEESE
3/4	CUP CELERY, FINELY CHOPPED
1/2	CUP SHREDDED CHEDDAR CHEESE
2	TBSPS. ONION, FINELY CHOPPED
1/4	TSP. SALT
2	4 OZ. PKG. HAM (8 SLICES)
1	LARGE DILL PICKLE

CUT BREAD LENGTHWISE; HOLLOW OUT EACH HALF WITH FORK LEAVING 1/2" THICK SHELL (SAVE INSIDES FOR BREAD CRUMBS). SPREAD MAYONNAISE OVER HOLLOWS; SPRINKLE PARSLEY OVER MAYONNAISE. BLEND CREAM CHEESE, CELERY, CHEDDAR CHEESE, ONION AND SALT AND SPOON INTO BREAD HALVES, PACKING DOWN WELL WITH BACK OF SPOON. LEAVE A SMALL HOLLOW DOWN THE CENTRE. QUARTER PICKLE LENGTHWISE. ROLL EACH QUARTER INSIDE A DOUBLE THICK SLICE OF HAM. PLACE ROLLS, END TO END, IN CENTRE OF HALF OF BREAD AND TOP WITH OTHER HALF. WRAP LOAF TIGHTLY IN TRANSPARENT WRAP. CHILL SEVERAL HOURS. TO SERVE, CUT INTO 16 SLICES.

SUNDAY SANDWICHES

IF THE QUEEN SHOULD HAPPEN TO DROP IN, YOU CAN IMPRESS HER WITH MORE THAN JUST A GRILLED CHEESE! FOR ONE SERVING.

- 2 SLICES BUTTERED BREAD
- 1 PROCESSED CHEESE SLICE (NOT WHITE)
  MAYONNAISE
  SLICED TOMATOES
- 1 EGG, BEATEN WITH A LITTLE MILK
  (GOOD FOR 2 SANDWICHES)
  SALT AND PEPPER
  BUTTER

SPREAD MAYONNAISE OF EACH SLICE OF BUTTERED BREAD. ADD CHEESE SLICE, TOP WITH SLICED TOMATOES AND SPRINKLE LIBERALLY WITH SALT AND PEPPER. PUT TOP ON SANDWICH. BEAT EGG WITH MILK AND POUR ONTO LARGE PLATE. DIP BOTH SIDES OF SANDWICH INTO MIXTURE AND COOK BOTH SIDES ON BUTTERED GRILL UNTIL CHEESE MELTS. SERVE WITH KETCHUP OR YOUR FAVORITE RELISH.

A BATH IS SOMETHING YOU TAKE WHEN YOU FIND YOURSELF IN HOT WATER.

EGGS RANCHERO

4	SPANISH ONIONS, THINLY SLICED
2	4 OZ. CANS DICED GREEN CHILIES, (EL PASO)
½	TSP. CUMIN
6	TBSPS. BUTTER
2	6 OZ. PKG. MONTEREY JACK CHEESE SLICES

8 TO 12 EGGS

PREHEAT OVEN TO 350°. SAUTÉ ONIONS IN BUTTER IN LARGE FRYING PAN UNTIL THEY ARE TRANSPARENT. ADD RINSED, DICED CHILIES AND CUMIN. SPREAD ONIONS IN 9" × 13" SHALLOW CASSEROLE. PLACE SLICES OF CHEESE OVER ONIONS. PUT IN OVEN TO MELT CHEESE (10 MINUTES). WITH FORK PULL AWAY MIXTURE TO MAKE NESTS AND BREAK ONE EGG IN EACH. SALT AND PEPPER TO TASTE. RETURN TO OVEN AND BAKE EGGS 8 TO 10 MINUTES UNTIL SET. SERVE ON TOASTED ENGLISH MUFFINS OR FOR THE MEXICAN TOUCH, ON TORTILLAS WITH REFRIED BEANS AND CHILI SAUCE.

TALK ABOUT CYNICAL. MY WIFE NOT ONLY DOESN'T BELIEVE THE STORIES IN THE NEWSPAPERS, SHE DOUBTS THE PHOTOGRAPHS.

Chicken Scramble

½ cup onion, chopped
½ cup green pepper, chopped
⅓ cup slivered almonds
¼ cup butter
2½ cups cooked chicken
¾ tsp. salt
  dash pepper
6 slightly beaten eggs
½ cup grated Parmesan cheese

In medium frying pan cook onion, green pepper and almonds in butter until vegetables are tender but not brown. Add chicken, salt and pepper. Mix well. Cover and cook until chicken is heated through (2 to 3 minutes). Combine eggs and cheese; pour over chicken. Cook and stir gently over low heat until done (7 to 10 minutes). Serves 6.

I have the most frustrated pet in the world — a turtle that chases cars!

CHRISTMAS MORNING WIFE SAVER

SUPERB! MAKE THE DAY BEFORE AND POP IT IN THE OVEN IN THE MORNING. SERVES 8. (SEE PICTURE).

16	SLICES WHITE BREAD, WITH CRUSTS REMOVED
	SLICES OF CANADIAN BACK BACON OR HAM
	SLICES OF SHARP CHEDDAR CHEESE
6	EGGS
½	TSP. SALT
½	TSP. PEPPER
½ TO 1	TSP. DRY MUSTARD
¼	CUP MINCED ONION
¼	CUP GREEN PEPPER, FINELY CHOPPED
1 TO 2	TSP. WORCESTERSHIRE SAUCE
3	CUPS WHOLE MILK
	DASH RED PEPPER (TABASCO)
¼	LB. BUTTER
	SPECIAL K OR CRUSHED CORN FLAKES

IN A 9" × 13" BUTTERED, GLASS BAKING DISH, PUT 8 PIECES OF BREAD. ADD PIECES TO COVER DISH ENTIRELY. COVER BREAD WITH SLICES OF BACK BACON, SLICED THIN. LAY SLICES OF CHEDDAR CHEESE ON TOP OF BACON AND THEN COVER WITH SLICES OF BREAD TO MAKE IT LIKE A SANDWICH. IN A BOWL, BEAT EGGS, SALT AND PEPPER.

THIS RECIPE CONTINUED PAGE 34.

CHRISTMAS MORNING WIFE SAVER

CONTINUED FROM PAGE 33.

TO THE EGG MIXTURE ADD DRY MUSTARD, ONION, GREEN PEPPER, WORCESTERSHIRE SAUCE, MILK AND TABASCO. POUR OVER THE SANDWICHES, COVER AND LET STAND IN FRIG OVERNIGHT. IN MORNING, MELT 1/4 LB. BUTTER, POUR OVER TOP. COVER WITH SPECIAL K OR CRUSHED CORN FLAKES. BAKE, UNCOVERED, 1 HOUR AT 350° LET SIT 10 MINUTES BEFORE SERVING. SERVE THIS WITH FRESH, CUT-UP FRUIT AND HOT CINNAMON ROLLS.

TOASTED TOMATO CHEESIES

8	SLICES BACON - CUT IN HALF
4	ENGLISH MUFFINS
1	8 OZ. PKG. CHEESE SLICES
2	TBSPS. ONION, FINELY CHOPPED
1	TSP. WORCESTERSHIRE SAUCE
2 TO 3	LARGE TOMATOES, SLICED

COOK BACON CRISP. DRAIN AND KEEP WARM. HEAT BROILER. PRY MUFFINS APART WITH FORK AND LAY SIDE BY SIDE ON COOKIE SHEET. TOAST UNDERSIDES UNDER BROILER (LIGHTLY). REMOVE FROM OVEN, TURN UPRIGHT. TOP EACH WITH SLICE OF CHEESE. COMBINE ONION AND WORCESTERSHIRE AND PUT SMALL AMOUNT ON CHEESE. TOP WITH A TOMATO SLICE. BROIL UNTIL HOT AND BUBBLY. GARNISH WITH 2 PIECES OF BACON. SERVES 4.

BAKED EGGS

Nice luncheon dish or a day when you want to skip meat at dinner. Serve with a salad.

1½	doz. eggs
¼	cup milk or cream
1	tsp. salt
1	10 oz. can mushroom soup
2	cans mushrooms
¼	lb. cheddar cheese

Add milk and salt to eggs. Beat and scramble until soft. <u>Don't overcook</u>! Mix soup and mushrooms together. Spray a 9" x 13" casserole dish with Pam or grease with butter. Put eggs in pan and pour soup mixture over. Sprinkle grated cheese or lay slices on top. Bake at 350° for 30 minutes. Cut into squares and serve hot. Serves 8 to 10.

Golf is like sex: when it's good, it's terrific, and when it's bad, it's still pretty good.

Cheese Soufflé

¼ Cup Quick Cooking Tapioca
1 Tsp. Salt
1⅓ Cups Milk
1 Cup Grated Cheddar Cheese
4 Egg Whites
4 Egg Yolks

Combine tapioca, salt and milk in saucepan. Cook and stir over medium heat until mixture comes to a boil. Remove from heat. Add cheese, stirring until melted. Cool slightly while beating egg whites until stiff. Beat egg yolks until thick and lemon coloured. Add tapioca mixture to yolks and mix well. Fold into egg whites. Pour into 1½ quart casserole. Set in pan of hot water and bake at 350° for 40 minutes or until firm. Serve at once. Serves 4 to 6.

The best way to remember your wife's birthday is to forget it once.

Christmas Marmalade

A friend once left this on my doorstep Christmas Eve (it was a warm night!) and I've made it ever since. Why not make a batch for your friends? Makes 7 - 12 oz. jars.

3	medium oranges
2	lemons
1½	cups cold water
1	6 oz. bottle preserved ginger
6	cups sugar
1	6 oz. bottle maraschino cherries, drained and chopped.
	Add extra green cherries as well— colourful!
½	bottle certo

Wash oranges and lemons. Slice paper thin. Discard seeds. Put into large kettle. Add water and bring to a boil. Turn down heat, cover and simmer about 30 minutes or until rinds are tender and transparent. Stir occasionally. Drain ginger, saving syrup. Chop ginger finely. Add sugar, chopped ginger, ginger syrup and cherries to orange-lemon mixture. Turn heat to high and bring to a full, rolling boil, stirring constantly. Boil hard one minute. Remove from heat and stir in certo. Continue stirring and skimming for 5 minutes. Ladle into hot, sterilized jars and seal with a thin layer of paraffin wax. (see picture).

THE MAYOR'S WIFE'S BLUE PLUM RELISH

A constant favorite that goes with practically everything. (Sunday sandwiches, Christmas morning "wifesaver".)

5	lbs. fresh, blue prune plums
3	large onions
4	lbs. cooking apples, peeled
1	qt. vinegar
4	lbs. white sugar
1/2	lb. preserved or candied ginger, grated
1	heaping tbsp. allspice
1	heaping tbsp. ground cloves
2	tbsps. cornstarch dissolved in...
1/4	cup water
	salt and pepper.

Pit and mince prune plums and grate onion and cooking apples. Place in large pot, add vinegar and boil together for 1/2 hour. Add sugar and bring to boil again. Simmer at least 15 minutes. Add ginger and continue to simmer at least 15 minutes more. Just before removing from heat, add allspice, ground cloves and dissolved cornstarch. Salt and pepper to taste. Pour into sterilized jars. Makes six quarts. Best aged 3 to 6 months.

A BOILED EGG IS HARD TO BEAT!

II BEST BUFFETS

Artichoke Nibblers

DELICIOUS AND CAN BE REHEATED.

2	6 oz. JARS MARINATED ARTICHOKE HEARTS
1	SMALL ONION, FINELY CHOPPED
1	CLOVE GARLIC, MINCED
4	EGGS, BEATEN
1/4	CUP FINE DRY BREAD CRUMBS
1/4	TSP. SALT
1/8	TSP. EACH PEPPER, OREGANO AND TABASCO
1/2	LB. SHARP CHEDDAR CHEESE, GRATED
2	TBSPS. PARSLEY
1	SMALL JAR PIMENTO (OPTIONAL)

DRAIN LIQUID FROM JAR OF ARTICHOKE HEARTS AND DISCARD. DRAIN LIQUID FROM THE OTHER JAR INTO FRY PAN. ADD ONION AND GARLIC AND SAUTÉ. CHOP ARTICHOKES INTO QUARTERS. COMBINE EGGS, CRUMBS, SALT, PEPPER, OREGANO AND TABASCO. STIR IN CHEESE, PIMENTO AND ARTICHOKES. ADD ONION MIXTURE. POUR INTO 7" x 11" BUTTERED BAKING DISH. SPRINKLE WITH PARSLEY. BAKE AT 325° FOR 30 MINUTES OR UNTIL LIGHTLY SET. COOL AND CUT IN 1" SQUARES.

ALL THINGS BEING EQUAL, YOU'RE BOUND TO LOSE.

CRAB MOUSSE

AN ELEGANT HORS D'OEUVRE MADE IN A 4 CUP MOLD.

- 1   10 OZ. CAN CREAM OF MUSHROOM SOUP
- 1   6 OZ. PKG. CREAM CHEESE
- 1   ENVELOPE GELATIN
- ¼   CUP COLD WATER
- ½   CUP FINELY CHOPPED CELERY
- ½   CUP FINELY CHOPPED GREEN ONIONS
- 1   CUP MAYONNAISE
- 1   5 OZ. TIN CRABMEAT
- ¼   TSP. CURRY POWDER

HEAT MUSHROOM SOUP AND CREAM CHEESE, STIRRING UNTIL SMOOTH. ADD GELATIN TO COLD WATER AND SOFTEN 5 MINUTES. ADD GELATIN MIXTURE TO SOUP MIXTURE. ADD CELERY, ONION, MAYONNAISE, CRABMEAT AND CURRY POWDER, MIXING WELL. POUR INTO 4 CUP COLD MOLD (OIL OR SPRAY MOLD WITH PAM BEFOREHAND). CHILL OVERNIGHT. UNMOLD ONTO SERVING PLATE AND DECORATE WITH SPRIGS OF FRESH PARSLEY. SERVE WITH CRACKERS.

MAY YOUR LIFE BE LIKE A ROLL OF TOILET PAPER — LONG AND USEFUL.

Curried Seafood Cocktail Puffs

SHELLS:

½	CUP	BUTTER
1	CUP	BOILING WATER
½	TSP.	SALT
1	CUP	FLOUR
4	EGGS	

SEAFOOD FILLING:

1 CAN (7 oz.) CRAB OR SHRIMP

⅓ CUP MAYONNAISE

1 TO 2 TSPS. CURRY POWDER (TO TASTE)

2 TBSPS. CHOPPED GREEN ONION

Preheat oven to 400°. In medium saucepan, heat butter with boiling water until butter is melted. Turn heat to low, add flour and salt, stirring vigorously until mixture forms smooth ball. Remove from heat and add eggs one at a time, beating well with a spoon after each addition. Drop by teaspoonfuls onto lightly greased cookie sheet and bake 20 to 25 minutes until golden. Cool, cut in half. Mix all ingredients for seafood filling together, and fill puffs, replacing tops. Heat before serving. Puffs can be made ahead and frozen.

CURRIED SCALLOPS

1	LB. SCALLOPS (FRESH OR FROZEN)
1/3	CUP VERY FINE BREAD CRUMBS
1	TSP. SALT
3	TBSPS. BUTTER
1	TSP. CURRY POWDER
2	TSPS. LEMON JUICE

BUTTER A LARGE BAKING DISH AND PREHEAT OVEN TO 450°. RINSE SCALLOPS UNDER COLD WATER AND DRY WELL ON PAPER TOWELLING. CUT EACH SCALLOP IN HALF AND ROLL IN BREAD CRUMBS. PLACE ONE LAYER IN BAKING DISH AND SPRINKLE LIGHTLY WITH SALT. MELT BUTTER IN SMALL SAUCEPAN, ADD CURRY AND COOK GENTLY FOR 2 MINUTES. STIR IN LEMON JUICE AND DRIZZLE THIS MIXTURE OVER SCALLOPS. BAKE 15 TO 20 MINUTES, UNTIL SCALLOPS ARE TENDER. SERVE IMMEDIATELY WITH COCKTAIL PICKS.

NEVER MIND THE JONESES, OUR FAMILY WOULD BE HAPPY TO KEEP UP WITH THE WALTONS.

HOT CHEESE SPREAD

- 3 CUPS GRATED SHARP CHEESE
- 1 SMALL CAN CHOPPED RIPE OLIVES
- 1 MEDIUM ONION, CHOPPED
- 1 CUP KRAFT MAYONNAISE
- ½ TSP. CURRY POWDER
  DASH OF GARLIC SALT AND PAPRIKA

MIX CHEESE, OLIVES AND ONION TOGETHER. ADD MAYONNAISE, CURRY POWDER, GARLIC SALT AND PAPRIKA. STORE IN REFRIGERATOR AND USE WHEN NEEDED. SPREAD ON PARTY RYE BREAD OR SMALL CIRCLES OF THIN BROWN BREAD OR TRISCUITS. HEAT UNDER BROILER UNTIL MELTED. ALSO GREAT WITH COFFEE CAN BREAD PAGE 17. (SEE PICTURE).

CURRY DIP FOR VEGETABLE PLATTER

- 1 CUP MAYONNAISE
- ½ CUP KETCHUP
- 1 TBSP. CURRY POWDER
  (MORE OR LESS, TO YOUR TASTE)
- 1 TBSP. WORCESTERSHIRE SAUCE
- 1 TSP. SALT
- 1 TSP. PEPPER

MIX ALL TOGETHER AND CHILL FOR A COUPLE OF HOURS. THIS WILL KEEP IN COVERED CONTAINER FOR A FEW DAYS.

Ha' Pennies- God Bless You

THIS IS A COCKTAIL COOKIE AND DOUBLES VERY WELL. A SPECIAL FAVORITE WITH THE LADIES.

- ½ CUP BUTTER
- 1 CUP FLOUR
- 8 OZ. GRATED CHEDDAR CHEESE
- 3 TBSPS. ONION "SOUP IN A MUG" OR ONION SOUP MIX

MIX ALL TOGETHER AND KNEAD UNTIL THOROUGHLY MIXED. ROLL INTO A LOG, WRAP IN WAX PAPER. CHILL. WHEN READY TO BAKE, SLICE IN ¼" THICKNESS AND PLACE ON AN UNGREASED COOKIE SHEET. BAKE AT 350° FOR 20 TO 25 MINUTES. THESE FREEZE WELL FOR UP TO 8 MONTHS, COOKED OR UNCOOKED. YIELDS: 12 TO 18.

WHAT THIS COUNTRY REALLY NEEDS IS A SHOPPING CART WITH WHEELS THAT ALL GO IN THE SAME DIRECTION.

JOHNNY'S MOMMY'S PATÉ

½	ENVELOPE GELATIN
1	CUP CONDENSED CONSOMMÉ SOUP
1½	CUPS CHICKEN FAT OR BUTTER
6	TBSPS. FINELY MINCED ONION
2	TSPS. SALT
½	TSP. NUTMEG
¼	TSP. GROUND CLOVES
¼	TSP. CAYENNE PEPPER
2	TSPS. DRY MUSTARD
1½	LBS. CHICKEN LIVERS

PUT ½ ENVELOPE OF GELATIN IN CONSOMMÉ. LET STAND 5 MINUTES, THEN STIR AND HEAT UNTIL GELATIN IS DISSOLVED. POUR INTO GLASS MEAT LOAF MOLD WHICH HAS BEEN SPRAYED WITH A "NO-STICK" PRODUCT. CHILL UNTIL SET. MEANWHILE, MIX BUTTER, ONION, SALT, NUTMEG, CLOVES, CAYENNE AND DRY MUSTARD IN A BLENDER OR FOOD PROCESSOR. CUT AWAY EXCESS FAT FROM CHICKEN LIVERS AND SIMMER IN ¼ CUP WATER FOR 15 TO 20 MINUTES (COVERED). DRAIN AND ADD TO MIXTURE IN BLENDER ONE OR TWO AT A TIME WHILE STILL HOT. WHEN EVERYTHING IS BLENDED, AND HAS A VERY SMOOTH TEXTURE, PLACE GENTLY ON ASPIC WHICH HAS SET. CHILL. TO UNMOLD, PLACE BRIEFLY IN HOT WATER. THIS AMOUNT WILL SERVE A COCKTAIL PARTY OF 50. ANY LEFTOVER MAY BE FROZEN. TO FREEZE, SCRAPE OFF ASPIC. WHEN READY TO USE AGAIN, PUT THAWED PATÉ IN BLENDER. REMOLD AND CHILL.

Lobster Dip

This dip is served warm in a chafing dish with a variety of crackers. (See picture).

2	TBSPS. CHOPPED GREEN ONION
2	TBSPS. CHOPPED GREEN PEPPER
2	TBSPS. BUTTER
1	10 oz. CAN MUSHROOM SOUP
1/2	CUP CREAM
1	TBSP. CORNSTARCH
2	TBSPS. SHERRY
2	EGG YOLKS
1/8	TSP. NUTMEG
2	5 1/2 oz. CANS LOBSTER
1	CUP GRATED CHEDDAR CHEESE

Sauté onion and green pepper in butter for 5 minutes. In separate saucepan, mix soup, cream, cornstarch, sherry, yolks and nutmeg. Heat slowly until it starts to thicken, add onion and green pepper; continue cooking until thick. Add cheese and lobster chunks, stirring well until cheese melts. Transfer to chafing dish and keep warm over low flame, uncovered. Makes 3 1/2 cups.

THE RESORT WAS SO DULL, ONE DAY THE TIDE WENT OUT AND NEVER CAME BACK.

PICTURED ON OVERLEAF:

APPETIZERS

Ham and Cheese Ball

Yummy hors d'oeuvre or casual afternoon snack. Serve with crackers. (See Picture).

8	oz. pkg. cream cheese
1/4	cup mayonnaise
2	8 oz. tins Burns flaked ham
2	tbsps. chopped parsley
1	tsp. minced onion
1/4	tsp. dry mustard
1/4	tsp. tabasco
1/2	cup chopped walnuts

Beat cheese and mayonnaise until smooth. Stir in next 5 ingredients. Cover and chill several hours. Form into two medium sized balls. Roll in nuts to coat. Freezes well.

His swimming pool burned down.

Crunchy Shrimp

Large frozen shrimp
Melted butter
Seasoned bread crumbs

Thaw peeled, cleaned and deveined shrimp. Dip in butter and roll in bread crumbs. Bake on a cookie sheet at 500° for about 10 minutes.

Mad Madeleine's Cheese Puffs

2   THIN SLICED SANDWICH LOAVES,
        DAY OLD (SKYLARK BREAD IF POSSIBLE)
1   LB. VELVEETA CHEESE
3/4 LB. BUTTER

WHIP SOFTENED CHEESE AND BUTTER UNTIL FLUFFY. TAKE 3 SLICES OF BREAD. SPREAD CHEESE MIXTURE ON EACH AND STACK. REMOVE CRUSTS. CUT INTO QUARTERS. ICE EACH PIECE ON SIDES AND TOP. YOU CAN USE A FORK THROUGH THE BOTTOM TO DO THIS. PLACE ON A COOKIE SHEET, COVER WITH FOIL AND FREEZE. WHEN READY TO USE, PREHEAT OVEN TO 350°. BAKE 10 TO 15 MINUTES UNTIL CHEESE MELTS. WATCH THEM CAREFULLY SO THEY DON'T BURN. MAKE SURE THE SQUARES ARE FROZEN BEFORE HEATING. THESE ARE REALLY DELICIOUS BUT QUITE FIDDLY TO MAKE. HOWEVER, BECAUSE THEY MUST BE FROZEN IN ADVANCE, THEY CAN BE MADE WELL AHEAD AND WILL KEEP IF CAREFULLY COVERED. MAKES 4 DOZEN.

I ALWAYS DO MY BEST THINKING OVER A GLASS OF BEER. TWO HEADS ARE BETTER THAN ONE.

Rumaki

A traditional hors d'oeuvre that's always a hit - even if you're not a liver lover. (See picture).

- Chicken livers - sold in 8 oz. cartons, but you'll only need half the amount
- 1 can water chestnuts - cut in half
- ½ lb. bacon strips - cut in half
- ½ cup soya sauce

Cut chicken livers into bite sized pieces and marinate in ¼ cup soya sauce for two hours. In another bowl, do the same with the water chestnuts. Wrap a piece of each in a strip of bacon (messy, but persist) and secure with <u>wooden</u> toothpick. Set on broiler pan and broil slowly, turning once, until bacon is crisp. Serves 6 to 8.

He was born with a silver spoon in his mouth, and every time he goes to a restaurant, he tries to complete the set.

Ruth's Chokes

These are fantabulous and so quick and easy. (see picture).

1 tin artichokes (14 to 16 count, if possible. If not available, use 8 to 10 count, cut in half)
½ cup Best Food Mayonnaise
½ cup Grated Parmesan cheese

Place artichoke hearts on cookie sheet. You may have to trim them a bit to get them to stand. Mix parmesan cheese in mayonnaise and top each artichoke with a teaspoon of mayonnaise mixture. Put under broiler for about 2 minutes or until top is browned. Watch constantly. These are great appetizers! Serve hot. Serves 4 to 6. <u>Note</u>: If large (8 to 10) artichokes are used, cut in half and rest on sides to broil.

Couple on their fiftieth wedding anniversary... She: "Why don't you bite me on the neck like you used to do?" He: "Okay, go get my teeth."

Purk's Poo-Poo's

MY KIND OF APPETIZER — A 24 HOUR MAKE AHEAD!

- 1 CUP MINCED RED ONION
- 3 CUPS GRATED SWISS CHEESE
- ¾ CUP MAYONNAISE

  SALT AND PEPPER TO TASTE

COMBINE ALL INGREDIENTS. ADD MORE MAYONNAISE TO MAKE A NICE SMOOTH SPREADING CONSISTENCY, IF NECESSARY. SERVE WITH TRISCUITS OR YOUR FAVORITE CRACKER. CHILL 24 HOURS BEFORE SERVING.

THE BEACH IS A PLACE WHERE A GIRL GOES IN HER BAITING SUIT.

Smoked Salmon Hors D'oeuvre
(SEE PICTURE)

- 1 8 OZ. PKG. CREAM CHEESE
- 1 TSP. CAPERS
- 1 TSP. CAPER JUICE
- 1 TSP. FINELY CHOPPED GREEN ONION
- 1 TSP. MAYONNAISE
- ½ LB. SMOKED SALMON OR LOX CUT INTO 1" STRIPS

CREAM FIRST FIVE INGREDIENTS. SPOON SMALL AMOUNT ONTO SALMON STRIP AND ROLL. FASTEN WITH COCKTAIL TOOTHPICKS. SERVES 6.

Sesame Cheese

The fastest hors d'oeuvre you ever made and delicious!

1   8 oz. pkg. cream cheese
1   tbsp. sesame seeds, toasted
1   tbsp. soya sauce

Unwrap cream cheese and set in shallow, small serving dish. Prick all over with toothpick. Sprinkle sesame seeds over cheese. Pour soya sauce over all. Spread on Melba toast, Triscuits or bacon dippers.

Success is relative. The more success, the more relatives.

Shrimp Dip

1   8 oz. pkg. cream cheese, softened
1/3   cup mayonnaise
2   tbsps. ketchup
2   tsps. chopped green onion
1/4   tsp. tabasco
1/2   to 3/4 lb. fresh cooked baby shrimp

Mix first five ingredients together and fold in shrimp. Serve with celery or crackers.

Soya Almonds

Something special for Christmas gifting.

- 1¼ lbs. blanched whole almonds
- ¼ cup butter
- ¼ cup soya sauce

Spread almonds in a 9"x13" baking pan. Toast at 400° for 15 mins. Stir often. Be Careful not to burn. Add butter and soya sauce and stir. Toast 12 to 15 mins. longer, or until nuts are coated and fairly dry. Cool and store in a jar. (See picture).

Caramelled Walnuts

- 1 lb. shelled whole walnuts
- 1 egg white
- 1 tsp. cold water
- 1 cup brown sugar
- ¼ tsp. salt

Beat egg white and water until frothy. Add walnuts and stir until well coated. Combine sugar and salt and cover walnuts. Bake 1 hour at 225° on a greased cookie sheet. Stir every fifteen minutes.

NOVEL NUTS

- 1 LB. LARGE PECAN HALVES
- 1 EGG WHITE
- 1 TSP. COLD WATER
- ½ CUP SUGAR
- ¼ TSP. SALT
- ½ TSP. CINNAMON
- SPRINKLE, FRESHLY GROUND NUTMEG

BEAT EGG WHITE AND WATER UNTIL FROTHY. ADD PECANS AND MIX UNTIL WELL COATED. COMBINE SUGAR, SALT, CINNAMON AND NUTMEG. ADD TO PECAN MIXTURE. BAKE 1 HOUR AT 225° ON BUTTERED COOKIE SHEET, STIRRING EVERY 15 MINUTES. THESE KEEP WELL IN A COVERED CONTAINER AND MAKE A LOVELY HOSTESS GIFT.

HEADLINE IN NEWSPAPER FOLLOWING ALFRED WONG'S UNSUCCESSFUL FLIGHT IN HOME MADE AIRPLANE: ONE WONG BANGED UP IN BID TO COPY TWO WRIGHTS.

Spiced Cashews or Pecans

A GREAT NIBBLER TO HAVE ON HAND WHEN YOU HAVE THE GROUP OVER TO PLAY CARDS.

2	CUPS NUTS (HALVES)
1½	TBSPS. MELTED BUTTER.
1	TSP. SALT
2	TSPS. SOYA SAUCE
⅛	TSP. TABASCO SAUCE

PREHEAT OVEN TO 300.° PLACE NUTS IN A JELLY ROLL PAN. MELT BUTTER AND POUR OVER NUTS. MIX REMAINING INGREDIENTS AND POUR OVER NUTS. BAKE 15 TO 20 MINUTES. STIR AND TOSS NUTS DURING COOKING TIME. COOL AND DIG IN — YUMMY! (SEE PICTURE).

MOST FAMILIES USE CREDIT CARDS FOR EVERYTHING — THE ONLY ONE WHO STILL PAYS CASH IS THE TOOTHFAIRY.

Tom's (Trail) Mix

2	CUPS RAISINS
1	CUP SHELLED SUNFLOWER SEEDS
2	CUPS CASHEW NUTS

MIX TOGETHER. ANY PROPORTION OF THESE INGREDIENTS MAY BE USED.

CRAZY CRUNCH

PUT THIS IN FANCY JARS AND GIVE IT AS A LITTLE EXTRA AT CHRISTMAS TIME.

2	QUARTS POPPED POPCORN
1⅓	CUPS PECANS
⅔	CUP ALMONDS
1⅓	CUPS SUGAR
1	CUP MARGARINE
1	TSP. VANILLA
½	CUP CORN SYRUP

MIX POPCORN, PECANS AND ALMONDS ON A COOKIE SHEET. COMBINE SUGAR, VANILLA, MARGARINE AND SYRUP IN A PAN. BOIL 10 TO 15 MINUTES OR TO A LIGHT CARAMEL COLOUR. POUR OVER CORN, PECANS AND ALMONDS. MIX WELL. SPREAD TO DRY.

THEY SAY CHILDREN BRIGHTEN UP THE HOME. THAT'S RIGHT - THEY NEVER TURN OFF THE LIGHTS.

Buffet Seafood Salad

1   LOAF WHITE SLICED BREAD
4   HARD BOILED EGGS
6   GREEN ONIONS, CHOPPED
1/4   LB. SOFT BUTTER
2   7 OZ. CANS CRAB
3   7 OZ. CANS SHRIMP
3   CUPS BEST FOODS MAYONNAISE

CUT CRUSTS OFF BREAD, BUTTER BOTH SIDES AND CUBE 1/2". CHOP EGGS AND ONION. PLACE BREAD CUBES, EGGS AND ONION IN PLASTIC BAG. LEAVE IN THE REFRIGERATOR FOR SEVERAL HOURS OR OVERNIGHT. WHEN PREPARING DINNER, DRAIN CRAB AND SHRIMP, PLACE IN LARGE BOWL WITH BREAD MIXTURE AND MAYONNAISE — MIX WELL. SERVE IN WOODEN BOWL OR PLATTER ON LETTUCE LEAVES. SERVES 12 TO 16.

THE MAN WHO WOULD RATHER PLAY GOLF THAN EAT SHOULD MARRY THE WOMAN WHO WOULD RATHER PLAY BRIDGE THAN COOK.

Pickled Cole Slaw

1	LARGE CABBAGE, FINELY CHOPPED
2	LARGE ONIONS, THINLY SLICED
¾	CUP SUGAR
1	TSP. SALT
1	CUP WHITE VINEGAR
2	TSPS. PREPARED MUSTARD
¼	CUP SUGAR
3	TSPS. CELERY SEED
¾	CUP SALAD OIL

Toss cabbage, onion, ¾ cup sugar and salt. Let stand while making the dressing.

Mix vinegar, mustard, ¼ cup sugar and celery seed in saucepan. Bring to a boil. Add oil. While bubbling, pour over cabbage mixture. Stir. Chill overnight. This will keep several weeks in the refrigerator. Serves 20.

THE BEST WAY TO REMOVE COFFEE STAINS FROM A SILK BLOUSE IS WITH A PAIR OF SCISSORS.

CANLIS' SPECIAL SALAD

ORIGINATED BY CANLIS' RESTAURANT IN HONOLULU.

THE SALAD

- 2 HEADS ROMAINE LETTUCE
- 2 PEELED TOMATOES
- 1 CLOVE GARLIC
- SALT
- 2 TBSPS. OLIVE OIL

THE CONDIMENTS

- 1/4 CUP GREEN ONION, CHOPPED
- 1/2 CUP ROMANO CHEESE, GRATED
- 1 LB. COOKED BACON-FINELY CHOPPED

THE DRESSING

- 3 OZ. OLIVE OIL
- JUICE OF 2 LEMONS
- 1/2 TSP. FRESH GROUND PEPPER
- 1/2 TSP. FRESH MINT, CHOPPED
- 1/4 TSP. OREGANO
- 1 CODDLED EGG
- 1 CUP CROUTONS

INTO A LARGE BOWL (WOODEN) POUR APPROXIMATELY 2 TBSPS. OF GOOD OLIVE OIL, SPRINKLE WITH SALT AND RUB WITH A LARGE CLOVE OF GARLIC. (THE OIL WILL ACT AS A LUBRICANT AND THE SALT AS AN ABRASIVE). REMOVE GARLIC. IN THE BOTTOM OF THE BOWL, FIRST PLACE TOMATOES CUT IN EIGHTHS; ADD ROMAINE LETTUCE, SLICED IN 1" STRIPS. CONTINUED NEXT PAGE!

Canlis' Special Salad

CONTINUED FROM PAGE 61.

NOTE: You may add other vegetables to this salad if you choose, but remember to put the heavy vegetables in first with romaine lettuce on top. Add condiments.

DRESSING

Pour the olive oil into a bowl, add lemon juice and seasonings. Add coddled egg and whip vigorously.

When ready to serve, pour dressing over salad. Add croutons last. Toss generously. Serves 6 to 8.

Cucumber Cream Salad

1	3 oz. pkg. lime Jello
1	tsp. salt
1	cup boiling water
2	tbsps. vinegar
1	tsp. grated onion
1	cup sour cream
½	cup mayonnaise
2	cups diced cucumber

Dissolve Jello and salt in boiling water. Add vinegar and onion. Chill until partially set. Blend in sour cream and mayonnaise. Fold in diced cucumbers and chill until firm. A light and refreshing treat.

Green Goddess Salad

THE NAME SAYS IT ALL!

Dressing

1	CLOVE MINCED GARLIC
1/2	TSP. SALT
1/2	TSP. DRY MUSTARD
1	TSP. WORCESTERSHIRE SAUCE
3	TSPS. GREEN ONION, CHOPPED
1	CUP MAYONNAISE
1/2	CUP SOUR CREAM
	TOUCH OF PEPPER

Salad

1	HEAD LETTUCE
2	TSPS. ANCHOVIES, CHOPPED
3	TSPS. PARSLEY, CHOPPED
1	CUP SHRIMP OR CRAB, COOKED
2	TOMATOES, QUARTERED

MIX INGREDIENTS FOR DRESSING TOGETHER AND CHILL. PREPARE SALAD AND TOSS GENTLY. POUR DRESSING OVER SALAD AND TOSS AGAIN, COATING WELL. DELICIOUS SERVED WITH A BUFFET OR LUNCHEON ALONG WITH WARM ROLLS.

SHE WENT ON A 14 DAY DIET, BUT ALL SHE LOST WAS TWO WEEKS.

LEE HONG'S CUCUMBERS

- 3 TBSPS. SALT (APPROXIMATELY)
- 1 CUCUMBER, SLICED VERY THIN
- 3 TBSPS. SUGAR
- 2 TBSPS. VEGETABLE OIL
- 1 THINLY SLICED SPANISH ONION
- 4 TBSPS. WHITE VINEGAR
- 4 TBSPS. WATER

ARRANGE CUCUMBER SLICES IN A BOWL IN LAYERS, SALTING BETWEEN LAYERS. LET STAND 2 HOURS. STAND BOWL UNDER FAUCET AND LET COOL WATER RUN THROUGH GENTLY UNTIL NO SALT REMAINS. DRAIN WELL. ADD SUGAR AND OIL. MIX AND ADD ONION, VINEGAR AND WATER. ADD MORE SUGAR OR VINEGAR IF NOT SWEET OR SOUR ENOUGH. RELISH SHOULD STAND A FEW HOURS BEFORE SERVING. GREAT WITH STEAK OR CHICKEN, HOT OR COLD MEAT. EXCELLENT!

AN ALARM CLOCK IS A SMALL MECHANICAL DEVICE TO WAKE UP PEOPLE WHO HAVE NO CHILDREN.

PICTURED ON OVERLEAF:

SALADS

FOO YUNG TOSSED SALAD

1 HEAD ROMAINE LETTUCE,
   (TORN INTO BITE SIZED PIECES)
1 1 LB. CAN, BEAN SPROUTS, DRAINED ...
   (OR USE FRESH BEAN SPROUTS)
1 5 OZ. CAN, WATER CHESTNUTS, SLICED
6 SLICES BACON, COOKED CRISP & CRUMBLED
2 HARD COOKED EGGS, SLICED
   SALT, TO TASTE
   PEPPER, TO TASTE
1 CAN, SHRIMP (OPTIONAL)

COMBINE ALL INGREDIENTS AND TOSS. ONCE YOU HAVE MADE AND TASTED THIS SALAD, YOU MAY USE YOUR IMAGINATION AND <u>ADD</u> DIFFERENT INGREDIENTS OR TRY CREAMY ITALIAN DRESSING. SERVES 6 TO 8.

DRESSING FOR FOO YUNG TOSSED SALAD

1/2 CUP SALAD OIL
1/3 CUP VINEGAR
2 TBSPS. SUGAR
1 TBSP. SOYA SAUCE
1/4 TSP. GROUND GINGER

IN SCREW TOP JAR COMBINE OIL, VINEGAR, SUGAR, SOYA SAUCE AND GINGER. SHAKE VIGOROUSLY, CHILL. JUST BEFORE SERVING, POUR OVER SALAD AND TOSS. (SEE PICTURE)

FIGHT TOOTH DECAY — EAT THROUGH YOUR NOSE.

SHRIMP LOUIS SALAD

Ladies love salads at noon and this should prove to be a popular one.

CREAMY MAKE-AHEAD DRESSING (1 1/3 cups)

1   cup cream style cottage cheese
1   hard cooked egg, peeled and halved
1/4   cup tomato juice
1   tsp. prepared mustard

Salad

1   lb. shrimp; cooked, peeled & deveined
1   large ripe avocado, peeled & sliced
1   cucumber, washed & unpeeled, sliced
1   large head of romaine lettuce
1   7 1/2 oz. tin ripe olives, halved

DRESSING

Combine cottage cheese, egg, tomato juice and mustard in container of electric blender. Whirl until smooth. Cover and chill until serving time.

SALAD

Combine shrimp, avocado, cucumber, olives and lettuce in large salad bowl. Toss gently and pour chilled dressing over. Toss again until well mixed. Accompany salad with a light chilled white wine and hot rolls. Yummy! Serves 8. (See picture).

"My garden's a little jewel - 14 carrots!"

Sunomono Salad Platter

Colourful, make ahead and different year 'round. (See picture).

Marinated Carrots

8	Medium carrots, peeled & grated
	Juice of 2 lemons
1	Tbsp. sugar
1	Tsp. salt

Sunomono

2	Large cucumbers, sliced paper thin
1/3	Cup vinegar
1	Tsp. salt
4	Tsps. sugar
1	Tbsp. water
2	Slices fresh ginger root, finely chopped....
or 1	Tsp. ground ginger

	Leafy lettuce
2	Cans green asparagus
2	Cans white asparagus
1/4"	Wide pimento strips
	Bottled Italian dressing
	Black pitted olives

See next page to put it together.

Sunomono Salad Platter

Continued from page 67

MARINATED CARROTS - Combine lemon juice, sugar and salt. Pour over grated carrots and marinate. Cover and chill for at least one hour.

SUNOMONO - Combine vinegar, salt, sugar, water and ginger. Pour over cucumber slices and marinate. Cover and chill for at least one hour.

To ASSEMBLE Salad Platter

Line a large platter with leafy lettuce. Drain and place cucumbers in small bowl and place in centre of the platter. Drain asparagus and place four of each colour on a lettuce leaf at 3" intervals. Slice pimento in 1/4" wide strips and place 2 or 3 over asparagus. Drain carrots and spoon between asparagus clumps. Place black olives at random around the edge of the platter. Carefully pour a small amount of Italian dressing on each bunch of asparagus. This can be made well ahead.

LET HIM WHO IS WITHOUT AIM THROW THE FIRST STONE.

Layered Salad

An amazingly fresh, crisp salad.
A different accompaniment to any meal.

1	Head iceburg lettuce, cut into bite sized pieces
1	Bunch fresh spinach, cut into bite sized pieces
1	10 oz. pkg. frozen peas (uncooked)
1	Bunch green onion, sliced
1	lb. crisp bacon, crumbled
5	Hard boiled eggs
1½	Cups mayonnaise

In a 9" x 13" pyrex dish, layer lettuce, spinach, peas, onions, sliced eggs and some bacon. Seal completely with mayonnaise. Refrigerate 24 hours. Sprinkle remaining bacon on top before serving. Serves 8 to 10.

Social tact is making your company feel at home, even though you wish they were.

Armenian Spinach Salad

1 Cucumber, thinly sliced
2 bunches fresh spinach
1 red onion, thinly sliced
½ cup Greek olives
1 cup feta cheese
Coarsely ground pepper

Dressing

⅔ cup grape seed oil, or olive oil
⅓ cup lemon juice

Wash, dry and tear spinach. Combine all salad ingredients in salad bowl. Combine oil and lemon juice in jar and shake well. Pour over salad and toss. Serves 4 to 6.

When your ship finally comes in, you will usually find relatives waiting at the dock.

Mandarin Orange Salad

1 CAN MANDARIN ORANGE SECTIONS, (DRAINED)
1 MEDIUM SIZED AVOCADO
1 HEAD BUTTER LETTUCE
  SLICES OF RED ONION (THIN)
  ITALIAN DRESSING

AT SERVING TIME, TEAR LETTUCE INTO BITE-SIZED PIECES IN SALAD BOWL. ADD ORANGE SECTIONS AND SLICES OF AVOCADO AND THIN SLICES OF RED ONION. TOSS WITH SALAD DRESSING. THIS IS A COLOURFUL, TASTY SALAD THAT SEEMS TO GO ALONG WITH ANY MEAL. (YOU MAY SUBSTITUTE ROMAINE LETTUCE FOR BUTTER LETTUCE.) (SEE PICTURE).

Salad Royale

1 CUP PITTED RIPE OLIVES, SLICED
3 CUPS FRESH SPINACH, HARD STEMS REMOVED
1/2 CUP SLICED FRESH MUSHROOMS
2 STALKS GREEN ONION, CHOPPED
1 TBSP. SESAME SEEDS (TOASTED)
8 CHERRY TOMATOES (OPTIONAL)
1/4 CUP CATALINA FRENCH DRESSING
1/4 TSP. CURRY POWDER

MIX FRENCH DRESSING AND CURRY POWDER. COMBINE FIRST SIX INGREDIENTS AND REFRIGERATE. JUST BEFORE SERVING, ADD DRESSING AND TOSS. SERVES 4 TO 6.

Turkey Soup

A meal in itself!

	Turkey Carcass, broken up
4	tsp. salt
2	chicken bouillon cubes
1	cup carrots, grated
1	cup celery, chopped
1	cup onion, chopped
1	20 oz. can tomatoes
4	tbsps. pot barley
1/4	cup lentils (dried vegetables)
2	tbsps. rice
1/4	cup parsley flakes
3	cups chopped turkey
1	cup macaroni or noodles (optional)

In a large kettle, place broken turkey carcass and bones in 18 cups of water and salt. Simmer 5 hours. Strain and discard bones. Place broth in refrigerator overnight to settle fat (it will lift off very easily). The broth will be jelly-like. Heat broth in large kettle. Add remaining ingredients and simmer 2 to 3 hours. Serve with bread and green salad.

An allowance is what you pay your children to live with you.

MINESTRONE SOUP

A MEAL IN ITSELF!! (NOT UNLIKE TURKEY SOUP).

1½	LBS. GROUND ROUND
1	CUP DICED ONIONS
1	CUP DICED ZUCCHINI
½	CUP DICED OKRA
1	CUP CUBED POTATOES
1	CUP SLICED CARROTS
½	CUP DICED CELERY
1	CUP SHREDDED CABBAGE
1	15 OZ. TIN TOMATOES
¼	CUP RICE OR . . .
	½ CUP MACARONI ELBOW NOODLES
1½	QTS. WATER
1	BAY LEAF
½	TSP. THYME
5	TSPS. SALT
	PEPPER TO TASTE
1	TSP. WORCESTERSHIRE SAUCE
½	CUP GRATED PARMESAN CHEESE

BROWN GROUND ROUND IN LARGE KETTLE.
ADD VEGETABLES, WATER AND SPICES AND BRING
TO BOIL. SPRINKLE RICE (OR NOODLES)
INTO MIXTURE. COVER AND SIMMER AT
LEAST ONE HOUR. SPRINKLE WITH GRATED
CHEESE. (SEE PICTURE).

CRAB AND CORN CHOWDER

WHAT COULD BE BETTER THAN CHOWDER, FRENCH BREAD AND WINE AFTER A DAYS' SKIING! CONSIDER THIS FOR CHRISTMAS EVE BUFFET.

1	SMALL ONION, CHOPPED
4	TBSPS. BUTTER
1/3	CUP FLOUR
3	CUPS MILK
2	MEDIUM POTATOES
1	SMALL GREEN PEPPER, CHOPPED
1	STICK CELERY, CHOPPED
1	BAY LEAF
1	CUP HALF & HALF CREAM
4	SLICES CRISP BACON, CRUMBLED
1	TBSP. PARSLEY
2	5 OZ. CANS CRABMEAT
1	7 OZ. CAN WHOLE KERNEL CORN

SAUTÉ ONION IN BUTTER UNTIL SOFT. ADD FLOUR, COOK GENTLY FOR 1 MINUTE AND REMOVE FROM HEAT. GRADUALLY ADD MILK. RETURN TO HEAT AND COOK UNTIL THICK. PEEL AND DICE POTATOES AND ADD WITH CHOPPED PEPPER, CELERY, BAY LEAF AND HALF & HALF CREAM. SIMMER 35 TO 40 MINUTES. ADD CRABMEAT, CORN, BACON AND HEAT THROUGH. SEASON WITH SALT AND PEPPER. GARNISH WITH PARSLEY. SERVES 4 TO 6.

CLAM CHOWDER

4	STRIPS BACON, DICED
1	SMALL ONION, CHOPPED
2	STALKS CELERY, CHOPPED
½	GREEN PEPPER, CHOPPED
1	CLOVE GARLIC, MINCED
1	BAY LEAF
2	10 oz. CANS CLAMS AND LIQUID
½	CUP WATER
2	CUPS RAW POTATOES, DICED
1	TSP. WORCESTERSHIRE SAUCE
¼	TSP. SALT
⅛	TSP. PEPPER
2	CUPS MILK

SAUTÉ BACON, ONION, CELERY, GREEN PEPPER AND GARLIC 5 MINUTES. ADD BAY LEAF, LIQUID FROM CANNED CLAMS, WATER, DICED POTATOES, SALT AND PEPPER. SIMMER UNTIL POTATOES ARE BARELY TENDER. ADD CLAMS, MILK AND WORCESTERSHIRE SAUCE. REMOVE BAY LEAF. SERVES 4.

SHE'S SO NEAT, SHE EVEN CHANGES THE PAPER UNDER THE CUCKOO CLOCK!

CRAB BISQUE

¼	LB. CRAB MEAT
3	TBSPS. SHERRY
1	10 OZ. CAN TOMATO SOUP
1	10 OZ. CAN GREEN PEA SOUP
1	CUP LIGHT CREAM
	SALT AND WHITE PEPPER TO TASTE

FLAKE CRAB AND SOAK IN SHERRY 10 MINUTES. BLEND UNDILUTED SOUPS AND SIMMER UNTIL HOT. ADD CREAM AND BLEND THOROUGHLY. ADD CRAB MEAT AND SEASONINGS. HEAT BUT DO NOT BOIL. SERVES 4.

IF YOUR WIFE WANTS TO LEARN TO DRIVE, DON'T STAND IN HER WAY.

CRAB CREAM SOUP

1	CAN MUSHROOM SOUP
1	CAN ASPARAGUS SOUP
1	CUP MILK
1	7½ OZ. TIN CRAB MEAT
1	TSP. WORCESTERSHIRE SAUCE
3	TBSPS. SHERRY
½	CUP WHIPPING CREAM

HEAT SOUPS AND MILK TOGETHER. ADD CRAB MEAT AND WORCESTERSHIRE SAUCE. STIR IN SHERRY AND FLUFF. STIR IN WHIPPING CREAM. SERVES 4.

CREAM OF CUCUMBER SOUP

A DELICIOUS COLD SOUP - MEN LOVE IT. MAKE THE DAY BEFORE. (YOU'LL NEED A BLENDER.)

2	8" ENGLISH CUCUMBERS, PEELED
2	TBSPS. BUTTER
1/4	CUP CHOPPED GREEN ONIONS
4	CUPS CLEAR CHICKEN BROTH OR...
	(5 BOUILLON CUBES DISSOLVED IN
	4 CUPS BOILING WATER)
1	TBSP. WINE VINEGAR
1/2	TSP. DRIED TARRAGON (OR MORE), CRUSHED
3	TBSPS. CREAM OF WHEAT (QUICK COOKING)
	SALT AND WHITE PEPPER
1	CUP SOUR CREAM

CUT 12 PAPER THIN SLICES OF CUCUMBER (SKIN ON) TO BE USED FOR GARNISH AND RESERVE. PEEL REMAINING CUCUMBER AND CHOP INTO CHUNKS. IN A LARGE POT, MELT BUTTER, STIR IN ONIONS AND COOK 1 MINUTE OVER MODERATE HEAT. ADD CUCUMBER CHUNKS, CHICKEN BROTH, VINEGAR AND TARRAGON. BRING TO A BOIL. STIR IN CREAM OF WHEAT. SIMMER, UNCOVERED, FOR 20 MINUTES. BLENDERIZE (IF TOO THICK, ADD SMALL AMOUNT OF CHICKEN BROTH OR MILK). SEASON TO TASTE WITH SALT AND WHITE PEPPER. LET COOL AND ADD SOUR CREAM TO SOUP IN BLENDER. SERVE WITH 2 SLICES OF RESERVED CUCUMBER ON TOP. SERVES 6.

HABITANT PEA SOUP

1½   LBS. DRIED YELLOW PEAS
½   LB. SALT PORK OR HAM BONE,
            (USE ANY SIZED BONE)
½   CUP DICED RAW POTATOES
1   DICED ONION
½   CUP CELERY, FINELY CHOPPED
⅛   TSP. THYME
       PINCH BASIL
       PINCH OREGANO
       SALT AND PEPPER TO TASTE
       SPRINKLE PARSLEY

SOAK PEAS IN COLD WATER AT LEAST 12
HOURS. RINSE WELL AND PLACE IN LARGE SOUP
POT. ADD 14 CUPS COLD WATER AND HAM BONE.
BRING TO A BOIL, SKIM OFF FOAM AND ADD
REMAINING INGREDIENTS. SIMMER OVER LOW
HEAT, COVERED, FOR 3 HOURS. ADD SALT AND
PEPPER TO TASTE. SPRINKLE WITH PARSLEY.
REMOVE BONE AND TAKE OFF MEAT. RETURN
MEAT TO SOUP. SERVES 12.

I ASKED HER IF I COULD SEE HER
HOME, SO SHE GAVE ME A PICTURE OF IT.

ELEPHANT SOUP

THIS HAS BEEN A BIG FAVORITE WITH OUR FAMILY. GREAT FOR LARGE "GRAY" CUP PARTIES, DEMOCRATIC CONVENTIONS. SERVES 50 SCORE.

1	MEDIUM ELEPHANT (AFRICAN IS BEST)
500	GALS. HOT WATER
2	PECKS ONIONS, FINELY CHOPPED
1	BUSHEL POTATOES, PEELED & SLICED
5	SHOVELS SALT
3	SHOVELS PEPPER
1½	CASES WORCESTERSHIRE SAUCE
10	BOTTLES RUM (OR MORE IF COOKING TIME IS LONGER OR YOU'RE EXPECTING MORE THAN 8 GUESTS.)
	COKE TO TASTE
5	QTS. PEANUT OIL (OPTIONAL) *

MIX 1½ OZ. OF RUM WITH COKE; DRINK. WASH AND DRY ELEPHANT (DON'T USE SOAP AS THIS WILL SPOIL FLAVOR.) CHOP INTO BITE SIZED CHUNKS. IN BACK OF ½ TON TRUCK (OR RENTED U-HAUL) POUR HOT WATER. HAVE ANOTHER RUM AND COKE AND ADD ELEPHANT, SPUDS AND OTHER INGREDIENTS. ALLOW TO SIMMER. MEANWHILE, FINISH FIRST BOTTLE OF RUM. STIR MIXTURE USING CANOE PADDLE OR SMALL OUT-BOARD MOTOR. WHEN GUESTS ARRIVE, START THEM OFF WITH REMAINING RUM. (* THE PEANUT OIL WON'T REALLY ADD TO SOUP, BUT IT'S THE WAY THE ELEPHANT WOULD HAVE WANTED IT!)

CORN SOUFFLÉ

A LOVELY CHANGE FOR CORN - ALWAYS GOOD WHEN SERVED WITH HAM. MUST BE PREPARED AND SERVED JUST BEFORE DINNER OR SOUFFLÉ WILL FALL. SERVES 4 TO 6. DON'T FORGET THE SALT!

1	10 OZ. CAN CREAMED CORN
4	EGGS
2	TBSPS. FLOUR
1	TBSP. SUGAR
2	TBSPS. BUTTER
1/4	TSP. SALT

SEPARATE EGGS INTO 2 MEDIUM SIZED BOWLS. BEAT TOGETHER YOLKS, SUGAR AND CORN. MELT BUTTER AND FLOUR, BEAT INTO CORN MIXTURE. BEAT EGG WHITES UNTIL STIFF AND FOLD INTO CORN. POUR INTO SOUFFLÉ DISH OR CASSEROLE. BAKE AT 350° FOR 45 MINUTES. SERVE AT ONCE.

SOME MEN NEED TWO WOMEN IN THEIR LIFE. A SECRETARY TO TAKE THINGS DOWN, AND A WIFE TO PICK THINGS UP.

PICTURED ON OVERLEAF:

SOUPS

MINESTRONE SOUP
    PAGE 73
FERGOSA
    PAGE 24

CREAMY WHIPPED POTATOES

This is a different twist to standard potatoes. Serve with steak, chicken or ham. Yummy! Serves 6 to 8.

8	MEDIUM POTATOES
1	TSP. SALT
1	PINT WHIPPING CREAM (2 CARTONS)
½	LB. GRATED SHARP CHEDDAR CHEESE

Boil potatoes with the salt. Mash and mix with ½ pint of whipping cream until thick and creamy. Add salt and pepper to taste and a sprinkle of the grated cheese. Put in a 9" x 13" casserole. Layer top with ½ pint cream WHIPPED; sprinkle grated cheese on top and bake at 300° for 1½ hours.

Dogs in Siberia are the fastest in the world, because the trees are so far apart.

CHEESY SCALLOPED POTATOES

THIS RECIPE CAN ALL BE MADE IN A FOOD PROCESSOR. SERVES 8.

6	MEDIUM POTATOES, PEELED AND SLICED
1/4	CUP DICED ONION
1/4	CUP CELERY LEAVES
2	SPRIGS PARSLEY
3	TBSPS. FLOUR
1/4	CUP BUTTER
1 1/2	TSPS. SALT
1/4	TSP. PEPPER
1 1/2	CUPS MILK
1 TO 2	CUPS GRATED SHARP CHEDDAR CHEESE
	DASH OF PAPRIKA

BLEND ONION, CELERY LEAVES, PARSLEY, FLOUR, BUTTER, SALT, PEPPER AND MILK IN BLENDER, MIXING THOROUGHLY. ARRANGE POTATO SLICES IN BUTTERED, 2 QUART BAKING DISH. POUR MIXTURE OVER POTATOES; SPRINKLE WITH GRATED CHEESE AND PAPRIKA. BAKE IN 350° OVEN FOR APPROXIMATELY 50 MINUTES. THIS CAN BE FROZEN AND REHEATED.

LOVE IS AN ITCH AROUND YOUR HEART THAT YOU CAN'T SCRATCH.

CASSEROLE PEAS

2	TBSPS. BUTTER
1/2	LB. FRESH MUSHROOMS, SLICED
2	10 OZ. PKG. FROZEN PEAS
1	10 OZ. CAN MUSHROOM SOUP, UNDILUTED
1	CAN BEAN SPROUTS, WELL DRAINED
1	4 OZ. CAN WATER CHESTNUTS, SLICED
	TOASTED SLIVERED ALMONDS, OR
	FRENCH ONION RINGS

HEAT BUTTER. ADD MUSHROOMS, SAUTÉ 5 MINUTES, COMBINE WITH PEAS, SOUP, BEAN SPROUTS AND CHESTNUTS. PLACE IN LIGHTLY BUTTERED CASSEROLE. BAKE AT 350° FOR 20 TO 25 MINUTES. PAT ALMONDS ON TOP OR MIX THEM IN OR PUT CHINESE NOODLES ON TOP. MAY BE WATERY BUT YOU CAN SERVE IT WITH A SLOTTED SPOON.

MOST WOMEN DON'T PLAY BRIDGE SKILLFULLY, BUT THEY ALWAYS PLAY FLUENTLY.

DEVILED CORN

GOOD FOR BUFFETS AND GOES WITH PRACTICALLY EVERYTHING. SERVES 6. BAKE AT 350° FOR ¾ HOUR BEFORE ADDING GARNISH.

4	TBSPS. BUTTER
2	TBSPS. FLOUR
1	TSP. DRY MUSTARD
1	TBSP. LEMON JUICE
½	TSP. SALT
	DASH OF PEPPER
½	CUP MILK
3	SLICES BACON, COOKED AND CRUMBLED
2	HARD COOKED EGGS, CHOPPED
1	14 OZ. TIN NIBLETS CORN, DRAINED
1	14 OZ. TIN CREAMED CORN
½	CUP GRATED PARMESAN CHEESE
½	CUP CRACKER CRUMBS
1	TBSP. BUTTER, MELTED
2	HARD COOKED EGGS, SLICED
	SLICED RIPE OLIVES, PITTED

IN LARGE SAUCEPAN, MELT BUTTER AND ADD FLOUR, MUSTARD, LEMON JUICE, SALT AND PEPPER. MIX WELL. ADD MILK AND STIR UNTIL THICK AND BUBBLY. REMOVE PAN FROM HEAT AND STIR IN BACON, CHOPPED EGGS AND BOTH TINS OF CORN. SPOON INTO 1½ QUART CASSEROLE AND SPRINKLE WITH PARMESAN CHEESE. COMBINE CRUMBS AND MELTED BUTTER AND SPRINKLE OVER CHEESE. GARNISH WITH EGGS AND OLIVES.

Easter Broccoli

This may be made ahead and heated through.

2   cups partially cooked broccoli,
    (fresh is best)
1   cup chopped celery
1   small jar pimento, chopped
1   10 oz. tin cream of mushroom soup
1   cup sour cream
    Grated cheese to cover

Mix soup and cream together. In separate bowl, mix vegetables. Pour soup mixture over vegetables and bake at 325° for 30 minutes. This recipe can be doubled, but cut down on sour cream, as it goes runny. Serves 6.

Popeye's Soufflé

2   10 oz. pkgs. chopped spinach,
     cooked and drained
1   egg, beaten
1½   cups sour cream
½   pkg. onion soup mix
1   cup grated cheddar cheese
¼   cup bread crumbs

Add egg to spinach, then mix in sour cream and soup mix. Pour into casserole dish. Cover with bread crumbs and cheddar cheese. Bake 40 minutes at 350°

TURNIPS 'N APPLES

EVERYBODY WHO TRIES THIS WANTS THE RECIPE — YOU'VE GOT IT! SERVES 6 TO 8.

1	LARGE TURNIP
1	TBSP. BUTTER
2	APPLES
1/4	CUP BROWN SUGAR
	PINCH OF CINNAMON

Crust

1/3	CUP FLOUR
1/3	CUP BROWN SUGAR
2	TBSPS. BUTTER

PEEL, DICE, COOK, DRAIN AND MASH THE TURNIP WITH BUTTER. PEEL AND SLICE APPLES. TOSS WITH BROWN SUGAR AND CINNAMON. ARRANGE, IN GREASED CASSEROLE, TURNIPS AND APPLES IN ALTERNATE LAYERS BEGINNING AND ENDING WITH TURNIPS. COMBINE CRUST INGREDIENTS TO A CRUMBLY TEXTURE AND PAT ON TOP OF CASSEROLE. BAKE AT 350° FOR ONE HOUR.

SHE TRIED TO BAKE A BIRTHDAY CAKE, BUT THE CANDLES MELTED IN THE OVEN.

Elsie's Potatoes

This can be made ahead and frozen.

5 lbs. potatoes or 9 large ones
1 8 oz. pkg. cream cheese, softened
1 cup sour cream
2 tsps. onion salt
1 tsp. salt
Pinch of pepper
2 tbsps. butter

Cook and mash potatoes very fine. Add all ingredients. Put into large greased casserole. Dot with butter. Bake, covered at 350° for 30 minutes. If making ahead, cover with plastic wrap and refrigerate or freeze. Thaw before baking. Serves 10 to 12.

The average girl would rather have beauty than brains, because the average man can see better than he can think.

FESTIVE MUSHROOMS

A VERY RICH DISH FOR SPECIAL OCCASIONS.
SERVE SMALL HELPINGS! GOOD WITH ROAST BEEF.

2	LBS. FRESH MUSHROOMS, CUT INTO "T's"
3	TBSPS. BUTTER
1	14 OZ. TIN PITTED RIPE OLIVES, SLICED
1	CUP GRATED, OLD CHEDDAR CHEESE
2	TBSPS. FLOUR
2	TBSPS. BUTTER
½	CUP SOFT BREAD CRUMBS
1	TBSP. MELTED BUTTER

SAUTÉ MUSHROOMS IN 3 TBSPS. BUTTER, UNTIL JUICY. IN A MEDIUM SIZED CASSEROLE, ADD A LAYER OF MUSHROOMS AND SLICED OLIVES. SPRINKLE WITH CHEDDAR CHEESE AND FLOUR; DOT WITH BUTTER. CONTINUE LAYERS IN THIS ORDER, AND TOP LAST LAYER WITH BUTTERED CRUMBS. BAKE AT 350° FOR 30 MINUTES. SERVES 8 TO 10.

AN IDEALIST IS ONE WHO, ON NOTICING THAT A ROSE SMELLS BETTER THAN A CABBAGE, CONCLUDES THAT IT WILL ALSO MAKE BETTER SOUP.

Green Bean Casserole

This recipe you can make ahead, set in the refrigerator and heat just before dinner. Try with ham or corned beef. Serves 8.

2	12 oz. pkgs. frozen french-cut beans, (cooked and drained)
1	5 oz. tin water chestnuts, drained, sliced
1/2	cup toasted, slivered almonds
1/2	cup butter
1	lb. fresh mushrooms, sliced
1	medium onion, sliced
1/4	cup flour
2	cups milk
1	cup cream
1 1/2	cups grated sharp cheddar cheese
1/8	tsp. Tabasco Sauce
2	tsps. Soya Sauce
1	tsp. salt
1/2	tsp. pepper

Sauté sliced onion and mushroom in butter. Add flour and mix. Add milk and cream, stir until thickened. Add remaining ingredients and simmer until cheese melts. Add cooked beans, mix well. Pour into greased shallow casserole. Sprinkle with toasted slivered almonds. Bake at 350° for 35 to 45 minutes.

MASHED POTATOES ALMONDINE

This casserole can be made a day ahead and kept in the refrigerator. Just heat before serving. A great accompaniment for any roast.

4	medium potatoes, cooked and mashed
1½	cups cottage cheese
¼	cup sour cream
2	tbsps. chopped green onion
1½	tsps. salt
	pepper to taste
2	tbsps. melted butter
¼	cup slivered almonds

Place cooked potatoes in large bowl and mash with electric beater. Add cottage cheese, sour cream, onion, salt and pepper. Beat until smooth and place in shallow casserole. Sprinkle with almonds and brush with melted butter. Bake at 350° for 30 minutes. Serves 6 to 8.

Many a women marries a man for life, and then finds out he doesn't have any.

Red Cabbage

Excellent with fowl! Serves 6 to 8.

1   3 lb. red cabbage
2   green apples, peeled and chopped
1   onion, finely chopped
¼   cup white sugar
¼   cup vinegar
2   tbsps. bacon fat
1   tsp. salt
      freshly ground pepper
½   cup boiling water

Shred cabbage. Put in saucepan with apples, onions, sugar, vinegar, bacon fat, salt and pepper. Stir until well mixed. Add ½ cup boiling water. Bring to boil and reduce heat. Cover and simmer 1 hour. Stir occasionally.

There is only one thing wrong with her face; it sticks out of her dress.

Rice Pilaf

Great with any meal! Can be frozen and re-heated with no ill effects.

- 1 cup Long Grain Rice
- 1 cup Pearl Barley
- ¼ cup Butter
- 8 Green Onions, chopped
- 2 10 oz. tins Consommé
- 2 tins Water
- 1 tin Whole Mushrooms with Liquid

Brown rice and barley in butter until golden, then add green onions, consommé, water and mushrooms with liquid. Cook either on top of stove in covered dutch oven for 30 minutes or in a covered casserole in 350° oven for one hour or until liquid is absorbed. Toss and serve. Serves 10 to 12.

All men are not homeless, but some are home less than others.

SAVOURY RICE

THIS CAN BE DOUBLED & TRIPLED. SERVES 4 TO 6.

1	TBSP. BUTTER
1	TBSP. ONION, CHOPPED
1	CUP CELERY
1	10 OZ. CAN CREAM OF MUSHROOM SOUP
1	10 OZ. CAN CONSOMMÉ
1	10 OZ. CAN CHICKEN WITH RICE SOUP
1	10 OZ. CAN MUSHROOMS, SLICED
½	CUP BLANCHED ALMONDS
1	CUP LONG GRAIN RICE

SAUTÉ ONION AND CELERY IN BUTTER UNTIL TRANSPARENT. PUT IN CASSEROLE. MIX ALL INGREDIENTS, EXCEPT ALMONDS. SAUTÉ THEM IN BUTTER. BAKE AT 300° FOR 45 MINUTES. COVER WITH ALMONDS. BAKE A FURTHER 30 MINUTES. THIS MAY BE KEPT WARM FOR A LONG TIME.

THE ONLY TIME SOME GIRLS DRAW A LINE IS WHEN THEY USE AN EYEBROW PENCIL.

SWEET POTATO SUPREME

GREAT WITH HAM! SERVES 4 TO 6.

- 2 CUPS MASHED, COOKED SWEET POTATOES
- 2 TBSPS. CREAM OR MILK
- 2 TBSPS. MELTED BUTTER

  SCANT TSP. SALT
- 1/4 TSP. PAPRIKA
- 1/2 CUP BROWN SUGAR, PACKED
- 1/2 CUP BUTTER
- 1 CUP (APPROXIMATELY) PECAN HALVES,
  TO COVER CASSEROLE

THOROUGHLY MIX POTATOES, CREAM, MELTED BUTTER, SALT AND PAPRIKA. SPREAD IN GREASED CASSEROLE. MAKE THE TOPPING BY HEATING BROWN SUGAR AND BUTTER OVER LOW HEAT, STIRRING CONSTANTLY, UNTIL BUTTER IS BARELY MELTED. (IT IS IMPORTANT NOT TO COOK AFTER BUTTER IS MELTED, OR THE TOPPING WILL HARDEN WHEN CASSEROLE IS HEATED.) SPREAD TOPPING OVER POTATOES AND COVER WITH PECAN HALVES. REFRIGERATE UNTIL READY TO HEAT. THIS CASSEROLE MAY BE WARMED IN AN OVEN OF ANY TEMPERATE OR MICROWAVE, BUT SHOULD BE BUBBLING HOT BEFORE SERVING. (SEE PICTURE).

WHEN LIFE HANDS YOU A LEMON— MAKE LEMONADE!

Schwarties Hash Browns

This freezes well and is great for buffets. Serves 8 to 10.

2	lbs. frozen hash browns
1	500 mL. carton sour cream
2	tins cream of mushroom soup
½	cup melted butter
	Grated onion and salt to taste
2	cups grated cheddar cheese
	Parmesan cheese

Thaw potatoes slightly for easier mixing. Mix first 6 ingredients in a 9" x 13" baking dish. Sprinkle parmesan cheese on top. Bake at 350° for 1 to 1½ hours.

Broccoli Rice Casserole

4½	cups cooked minute rice
1	10 oz. pkg. chopped broccoli
1	cup chopped celery
½	cup chopped onions
4	tbsps. butter
2	10 oz. tins cream of mushroom soup
1	cup milk
1	10 oz. jar cheese whiz

Cook rice and broccoli. Sauté celery and onion in butter. Combine soup, milk and cheese. Put all ingredients into a casserole. Bake at 350° for 40 to 50 minutes. Serves 12 to 16.

Sesame Broccoli ~~horrible~~

2	LBS. FRESH BROCCOLI
2	TBSPS. SALAD OIL
2	TBSPS. VINEGAR
2	TBSPS. SOYA SAUCE
8	TSPS. SUGAR
2	TBSPS. TOASTED SESAME SEEDS

POUR BOILING WATER OVER BROCCOLI AND LET STAND 5 MINUTES. DRAIN. HEAT ALL INGREDIENTS AND POUR OVER BROCCOLI IN CASSEROLE. HEAT IN OVEN BEFORE SERVING. SERVES 8. (SEE PICTURE).

Hot Curried Fruit

GOOD WITH BAKED HAM OR PORK. SERVES 6 TO 8. (SEE PICTURE).

1	CUP BROWN SUGAR
1/4	TSP. SALT
1	TBSP. CURRY
1/2	CUP BUTTER
3	14 oz. CANS FRUIT, DRAINED
	(CHOOSE A COMBINATION OF PINEAPPLE, PEARS, PEACHES, APRICOTS OR MANDARIN ORANGES)
	MARASCHINO CHERRIES FOR COLOUR.

COMBINE FIRST FOUR INGREDIENTS IN A SAUCEPAN AND BRING TO A BOIL. COOK 5 MINUTES. POUR OVER FRUIT IN BUTTERED CASSEROLE. BAKE AT 300° FOR 20 TO 25 MINUTES.

Turnip Puff

Ideal for those Thanksgiving and Christmas dinners when you'd like to serve your vegetables in a different, special way.

6	cups cubed turnips
2	tbsps. butter
2	eggs, beaten
3	tbsps. flour
1	tbsp. brown sugar
1	tsp. baking powder
3/4	tsp. salt
1/8	tsp. pepper
	pinch nutmeg
1/2	cup fine crumbs
2	tbsps. melted butter

Cook turnip until tender. Drain and mash. Add butter and egg. Beat well. (This much can be done the day ahead.) Combine flour, sugar, baking powder, salt, pepper and nutmeg. Stir. Butter a casserole dish and put in mixture. Combine crumbs and butter. Sprinkle on top. Bake at 375° for 25 minutes or until light brown on top. Serves 6.

Home cooking is what a man misses when his wife isn't.

YEAR ROUND GREENS

1	HEAD CAULIFLOWER, BROKEN INTO FLOWERETTES
1	CELERY HEART, CUT IN 2" DIAGONAL SLICES
2	STALKS BROCCOLI, BROKEN INTO FLOWERETTES
3	MEDIUM GREEN PEPPERS, CUT IN 2" SQUARES
4	TBSPS. OIL
1	SPANISH ONION, CUT IN SIXTHS
2	10 oz. CANS WHOLE MUSHROOMS
1½	TBSPS. LEMON JUICE
¼-½	CUP SOYA SAUCE

FILL 3 QUART SAUCE PAN ⅔ FULL WITH WATER, BRING TO BOIL AND PLACE CAULIFLOWER IN BOILING WATER. COOK 3 MINUTES, REMOVE AND SET ASIDE. PLACE CELERY IN BOILING WATER AND BOIL 3 MINUTES. REMOVE AND SET ASIDE. IN SIMILAR MANNER COOK BROCCOLI FOR 2 MINUTES AND GREEN PEPPER FOR 1 MINUTE. DRAIN VEGETABLES WELL. IN LARGE FRYING PAN OR WOK, HEAT OIL. ADD COOKED VEGETABLES, MUSHROOMS AND ONIONS. STIR FRY 2 MINUTES. POUR LEMON JUICE AND SOYA SAUCE OVER MIXTURE. COVER AND COOK OVER LOW HEAT 6 MINUTES OR UNTIL TENDER. SERVES 8 TO 10.

MY WIFE'S T.V. DINNERS MELT IN YOUR MOUTH. I WISH SHE'D DEFROST THEM FIRST.

ZUCCHINI CASSEROLE

1½	LBS. ZUCCHINI
4	EGGS
½	CUP MILK
1	LB. JACK OR MOZZARELLA CHEESE, GRATED
1	TSP. SALT
2	TSPS. BAKING POWDER
3	TBSPS. FLOUR
½	CUP BREAD CRUMBS
	BUTTER OR MARGARINE

PREHEAT OVEN TO 350°. WASH AND CUT THE ZUCCHINI INTO ½" SLICES. COOK IN A SMALL AMOUNT OF WATER UNTIL BARELY TENDER (5 MINUTES). DRAIN AND COOL. BEAT EGGS SLIGHTLY AND ADD MILK, GRATED CHEESE, SALT, BAKING POWDER AND FLOUR. STIR ZUCCHINI INTO EGG MIXTURE. PLACE IN BUTTERED CASSEROLE. SPRINKLE WITH CRUMBS AND DOT WITH BUTTER. BAKE FOR 35 TO 40 MINUTES.

TO BRING OUT THE FLAVOUR OF ZUCCHINI, CUT AND LET STAND IN A DISH OF SALTED WATER FOR 15 TO 30 MINUTES. SERVES 6.

WHAT A WONDERFUL NIGHT. THE MOON WAS OUT AND SO WERE HER PARENTS.

Broccoli Casserole

1	clove garlic, minced
1	large onion, chopped
¼	cup butter
4	cups broccoli, bite sized pieces
1	10 oz. tin cream of mushroom soup
1	7 oz. roll sharp cheese snack or
	7 oz. cheese whiz
1	tin sliced mushrooms, drained or
	¼ lb. fresh mushrooms (sauté with onions)
¼	cup chopped almonds
½	cup buttered bread crumbs
¼	cup chopped almonds

Sauté onion and garlic in butter. Spoon into large greased casserole. Cook broccoli until crunchy. Add to casserole. Add mushrooms and chopped almonds. In a separate bowl, blend mushroom soup and cheese. Fold into casserole. Top with almonds and buttered bread crumbs. Bake at 350° for 45 minutes. Serves 10.

One small boy to another — "Of course I know the facts of life; eat your vegetables and wash your hands."

Pickled Onions

I serve these with prime rib sandwiches. Easy for 8 or 80. Butter bread days ahead and freeze on trays. If you use large napkins no plates are necessary. Slice beef thinly!

4	large yellow onions, thinly sliced
1½	cups white vinegar
1½	cups water
1	cup white sugar
¼	cup lemon juice, fresh if possible
¼	tsp. Tabasco sauce
1	tsp. salt
½	tsp. seasoned pepper
2	cloves garlic, minced
1	cup sour cream
1	tsp. celery seed

Slice onions in very thin slices. Combine all ingredients except sour cream and celery seed. Marinate for 1, 2 or 3 days. Three hours before serving drain and stir-in sour cream and celery seed. Place in pretty bowl — there's nothing beautiful about an onion!

To prevent a head cold from going to your chest, just tie a knot in your neck.

SCAMPI
(SEE PICTURE)

¼ CUP BUTTER

¼ CUP SALAD OR OLIVE OIL

1 TBSP. GARLIC POWDER

1 TSP. SALT

DASH OF CAYENNE

2 TBSPS. LEMON JUICE

3 GREEN ONIONS, CHOPPED

1 LB. LARGE SHRIMP, PEELED & DEVEINED

PREHEAT OVEN TO 400°F. IN A LARGE OVENPROOF SKILLET OR SERVING DISH, COMBINE FIRST 7 INGREDIENTS, MELT AND MIX WELL. ADD SHRIMP AND COAT WITH BUTTER MIXTURE. BAKE 8 TO 10 MINUTES OR UNTIL TENDER. GARNISH WITH LEMON WEDGES. SERVES 4.

YOU GOTTA HAVE "SOLE"

4 SOLE FILLETS (OR ANY WHITE FISH)

½ CUP SOFTENED BUTTER

1 CUP GRATED PARMESAN

SPREAD HALF THE BUTTER IN A SHALLOW BAKING PAN. SPRINKLE ON HALF THE CHEESE. ARRANGE FILLETS IN SINGLE LAYER ON TOP, DOT WITH REMAINING BUTTER AND SPRINKLE ON THE REMAINING CHEESE. BAKE AT 400°, BASTING WITH MELTED BUTTER AND CHEESE UNTIL FISH FLAKES – ABOUT 15 MINUTES. SERVE WITH DRIPPINGS. SERVES 4.

Aunty Pasto's Seafood Lasagne

Twice as expensive and twice as good! A tasty variation of an old favorite. Freezes well. Serves 8 to 10.

8	Lasagne Noodles
2	tbsps. Butter
1	cup chopped Onion
1	8 oz. pkg. cream cheese, softened
1½	cups creamed Cottage Cheese
1	egg, beaten
2	tsps. Basil
½	tsp. Salt
⅛	tsp. Pepper
2	10 oz. cans Cream of Mushroom Soup
⅓	cup Milk
⅓	cup dry white wine or ....
	⅓ cup dry Vermouth
1	5 oz. can Crab
1	lb. shelled, deveined cooked Shrimp
¼	cup grated Parmesan cheese
½	cup shredded, sharp Cheddar Cheese

Cook noodles. Place 4 in 9" x 13" pan. Cook onion in butter. Add cream cheese, cottage cheese, egg, basil, salt and pepper.

This recipe continued page 104

Aunty Pasto's Seafood Lasagne

Continued from page 103
Spread ½ mixture over noodles. Combine soup, milk and wine. Stir in crab and shrimp. Spoon ½ mixture over cheese layer. Repeat all layers. Sprinkle with Parmesan cheese and bake, uncovered at 350° for 45 minutes. Top with sharp cheese, brown under broiler and let stand 15 minutes before serving.

Stuffed Arctic Char

1 whole Arctic char (5 lbs.), deboned as much as possible
1 cup softened butter
1 large onion, chopped
4 stalks celery, chopped
1 large green pepper, chopped
  Pimento - just to add some colour, sliced
  Salt and pepper to taste

Mix butter, onion, celery, green pepper, pimento, salt and pepper. Fill the fish cavity with mixture. Secure the fish by tying in several places with string. Rub generously with butter. Wrap in foil. Place in roasting pan on trivet and add enough water to cover the bottom (add more water as needed throughout cooking time). Bake for 50 minutes at 350°. Serves 6.

BAR-B-QUED SALMON STEAKS

IF THE FAMILY FISHERMAN HAS BEEN SUCCESSFUL, OR YOU HAVE BEEN GIFTED WITH (OH JOY, OH RAPTURE) A SALMON, TRY THIS.

SALMON STEAKS-CUT AT LEAST 1" THICK
1/2 CUP BUTTER
1 1/2 TSPS. SALT
2 TBSPS. LEMON JUICE
1 1/2 TBSPS. MUSTARD POWDER
PEPPER TO TASTE

COMBINE LAST 5 INGREDIENTS IN A SMALL BOWL. BAR-B-QUE SALMON ON GRILL 4" FROM HOT COALS FOR 6 TO 8 MINUTES EACH SIDE. DON'T OVERCOOK. BASTE FREQUENTLY WITH MIXTURE IN BOWL WITH A PASTRY BRUSH. SERVE WITH LEMON WEDGES, A HUGE GREEN SALAD AND FRENCH BREAD — MARVELOUS!

BRIDGE WEEKEND CONVERSATION:
"I WENT TO BED WITHOUT BRUSHING MY TEETH—I COULDN'T FIND MY TOOTHBRUSH." REPLY—"I COULDN'T FIND MY TEETH!"

Oyster Scallop

1	PINT OYSTERS, SLICED, PLUS LIQUID
2	TBSPS. MILK
1/2	CUP WHITE BREAD CRUMBS (DAY OLD)
1	CUP CRUSHED CRACKERS
1/2	CUP BUTTER, MELTED
	SALT AND PEPPER

IN A 1 QUART CASSEROLE ARRANGE, FIRST; A LAYER OF OYSTERS, THEN BREAD CRUMBS AND CRACKERS, THEN BUTTER AND MILK. REPEAT AND TOP WITH A LAYER OF CRUMBS. BAKE AT 350° FOR 30 MINUTES. SERVES 6.

Rice and Olive Stuffing for Salmon

THIS IS A SUPERB STUFFING FOR A 10 TO 12 POUND SALMON. IF THERE IS ANY LEFT OVER, WRAP IN FOIL AND COOK BESIDE FISH.

1/2	CUP BUTTER
1 1/2	CUPS MINCED ONION
2	CUPS DICED CELERY
2 2/3	CUPS COOKED RICE
2	CUPS CHOPPED STUFFED OLIVES
1/2	TSP. SALT
1/2	TSP. DRIED SAGE
1/2	TSP. PEPPER
1/2	TSP. THYME

THIS RECIPE CONTINUED PAGE 107

Rice and Olive Stuffing for Salmon

Continued from page 106

Melt butter in skillet. Sauté onion and celery until tender. Add rice and remaining ingredients. Toss. Spoon into cavity of fish (don't pack) and sew up with needle and thread. Messy job—but worth it! Spread a little butter (or a lot of mayonnaise) over fish, top with 3 or 4 lemon slices and wrap loosely in foil. Set in broiling pan and cook 10 minutes per inch of thickness at 425° (or until fork tender).

Serving Suggestion: Instead of serving with additional lemon wedges, make a sauce using equal proportions of melted butter and dry white wine.

Always get married early in the morning. That way, if it doesn't work out, you haven't wasted the whole day.

Chilled Salmon Soufflé

1½	ENVELOPES UNFLAVORED GELATIN
½	CUP COLD TOMATO JUICE
1	10 OZ. CAN CREAM OF SHRIMP SOUP
¾	CUP MILK
4	EGGS, SEPARATED
¼	CUP LEMON JUICE
1½	TSPS. PREPARED HORSERADISH
1½	TSPS. SALT
½	PINT WHIPPING CREAM
1	15½ OZ. CAN SALMON, DRAINED & FLAKED
1	TBSP. SNIPPED PARSLEY

SPRINKLE GELATIN OVER TOMATO JUICE AND LET STAND 5 MINUTES TO SOFTEN. ADD SOUP AND MILK AND HEAT TO A SIMMER, STIRRING CONSTANTLY, UNTIL GELATIN IS DISSOLVED. STIR A LITTLE OF THE HOT MIXTURE INTO WELL-BEATEN EGG YOLKS. RETURN TO SAUCE PAN AND COOK 2 MINUTES LONGER. ADD LEMON JUICE, HORSERADISH AND SALT. CHILL UNTIL PARTIALLY SET. BEAT EGG WHITES UNTIL STIFF BUT NOT DRY. WHIP CREAM UNTIL SOFTLY STIFF. FOLD EGG WHITES, CREAM AND SALMON INTO CHILLED MIXTURE. TURN INTO A 1 QUART SOUFFLÉ DISH WHICH HAS BEEN EXTENDED WITH A 2" PAPER COLLAR. CHILL UNTIL SET. REMOVE COLLAR AND GARNISH WITH PARSLEY. SERVES 6 TO 8.

Baked Sole Roulade

1½	LBS.	FROZEN RAW SHRIMP
1½	CUPS	SOFT BREAD CRUMBS
1		EGG, BEATEN
½	TSP.	JOHNNY'S SEAFOOD SEASONING
6		SOLE FILLETS
½	TSP.	SALT
2	TBSPS.	BUTTER
2	TBSPS.	LEMON JUICE
1	PKG.	"KNORR-SWISS" HOLLANDAISE -SAUCE MIX

Cook shrimp according to package directions. Drain and set 6 aside. Chop remaining shrimp and mix with bread crumbs, egg and seafood seasoning. Lay fish on wax paper; spread shrimp mixture evenly over each fillet. Roll up jelly-roll fashion and secure with toothpicks. Place seam-side down in baking dish. Sprinkle with salt and lemon juice. Dot with butter. Cover and bake at 350° for 30 minutes or until fish flakes easily. Prepare hollandaise sauce and keep warm. Lift fish carefully from baking dish and remove picks. Spoon part of hollandaise over the tops and garnish with set-aside shrimp. Serve remaining sauce separately. Serves 6.

Money talks, but it doesn't say when it's coming back

ALMOND CHICKEN

IF YOU HAVE A WOK IT WILL COME IN HANDY FOR THIS RECIPE. SERVES 4.

2	CHICKEN BREASTS
3	TBSPS. OIL
4	WATER CHESTNUTS
2	CUPS CHOPPED CELERY
1	CUP FRESH MUSHROOMS
1	CUP CHOPPED ONION
1	6 OZ. PKG. ALMONDS, SLIVERED
1 TO 2	TBSPS. DRY WHITE WINE
3	TBSPS. SOYA SAUCE
½	CUP WATER
2	TSPS. SALT
	DASH OF PEPPER
½	TSP. MINCED GARLIC
1	TBSP. CORNSTARCH

REMOVE SKIN AND BONES FROM CHICKEN. WASH, DRAIN AND DRY. DICE. SPRINKLE WITH WINE, PEPPER, AND SALT. DICE MUSHROOMS, CELERY, ONION AND CHESTNUTS. DRAIN, DRY AND MIX TOGETHER. SET ASIDE. HEAT FRYING PAN TO MEDIUM HEAT. ADD 1 TBSP. OIL. BROWN ALMONDS FOR 2 MINUTES. STIR CONSTANTLY. REMOVE FROM PAN. HEAT 1 TBSP. OIL, BROWN GARLIC SLIGHTLY. ADD CHICKEN. STIR AND TOSS 1 MINUTE. REMOVE FROM STOVE AND SET ASIDE. CONTINUED, PAGE 111.

ALMOND CHICKEN

THIS RECIPE CONTINUED FROM PAGE 110.
HEAT PAN WITH 1 TBSP. OIL ON HIGH. ADD
VEGETABLES. STIR FRY 3 MINUTES. SPRINKLE
WITH SOYA SAUCE. ADD WATER. COVER AND
COOK 3 MINUTES. THICKEN WITH CORNSTARCH
AND SPRINKLE WITH ALMONDS. SERVE WITH RICE.

SUMMER IS THAT TIME OF YEAR WHEN
CHILDREN SLAM THE DOORS THEY LEFT
OPEN ALL WINTER.

LEMON CHICKEN

SO EASY AND SO YUMMY. SERVES 4 TO 6.

4	WHOLE CHICKEN BREASTS (OR THIGHS)
½	CUP MELTED BUTTER
	SALT AND PEPPER (SPRINKLE TO TASTE)
½	TSP. THYME
1	LEMON, UNPEELED, THINLY SLICED

HALVE CHICKEN BREASTS AND ARRANGE IN
A 9" × 13" SHALLOW, BUTTERED, BAKING DISH.
SPRINKLE WITH SALT AND PEPPER AND THYME.
POUR MELTED BUTTER OVER ALL. ARRANGE
LEMON SLICES ON TOP OF CHICKEN TO COVER
ALL PIECES. COOK, UNCOVERED, FOR 1 HOUR
AT 350°. SERVE WITH RICE, VEGETABLES OR
SALAD.

BEEF & BURGUNDY CASSEROLE

AN ELEGANT STEW FOR 8 GOOD FRIENDS.

3	LBS. LEAN CHUCK OR ROUND STEAK, CUT IN 2" CUBES
2	TBSPS. BUTTER
2	TBSPS. BACON FAT
3	TBSPS. FLOUR
1/2	TSP. PEPPER
2	TSPS. SALT
1/2	TSPS. DRIED SWEET BASIL OR 1 1/2 TSP. FRESH CHOPPED BASIL
1	CLOVE GARLIC, MINCED
1/2	TSP. DRIED OREGANO OR 1 1/2 TSPS. FRESH CHOPPED OREGANO
1	LB. TINY WHITE ONIONS, PEELED & PARBOILED OR 1 LB. CAN
2	14 OZ. CANS BABY CARROTS
1	CUP BURGUNDY OR OTHER DRY RED WINE
2	TBSPS. BUTTER
1	TBSP. SUGAR
3/4	CUP MADEIRA WINE
1/4	CUP BRANDY

THIS RECIPE IS CONTINUED ON NEXT PAGE!

HE WHO LAUGHS LAST, USUALLY HAS A TOOTH MISSING.

BEEF & BURGUNDY CASSEROLE

FOR INGREDIENTS SEE PAGE 112.

HEAT BUTTER AND BACON FAT IN A LARGE, HEAVY SKILLET AND BROWN BEEF. PLACE IN LARGE CASSEROLE. ADD TO THE FAT; FLOUR, SALT, PEPPER, BASIL, OREGANO AND GARLIC. STIR UNTIL FLOUR BEGINS TO BROWN. DRAIN AND RESERVE LIQUID FROM VEGETABLES. ADD TO LIQUID ENOUGH WATER TO MAKE A SCANT 2 CUPS. ADD TO SKILLET AND STIR UNTIL THICKENED. ADD BURGUNDY AND STIR UNTIL SAUCE IS SMOOTH AND SOMEWHAT THICKENED. POUR OVER MEAT. COVER AND BAKE 3 HOURS IN A 300° OVEN. IN A SKILLET MELT BUTTER AND STIR IN SUGAR. WHEN THIS HAS MELTED, ADD DRAINED VEGETABLES AND STIR FREQUENTLY UNTIL SLIGHTLY BROWNED. ADD TO CASSEROLE WITH MADEIRA AND CONTINUE TO COOK COVERED FOR 30 MINUTES. STIR IN BRANDY JUST BEFORE SERVING. SERVE WITH RICE AND GREEN SALAD.

THE COST OF LIVING IS HIGH, BUT CONSIDER THE ALTERNATIVES.

CANNELLONI

PREPARE MINDLESS MEAT SAUCE AND CHICKEN FILLING AHEAD OF TIME AND THIS WILL SEEM EFFORTLESS. REGARDLESS, THE RESULTS ARE WORTH THE TIME INVOLVED. MAKES 20 CANNELLONI OR 10 SERVINGS.

CHICKEN FILLING

3	LARGE CHICKEN BREASTS, COOKED IN OVEN, RESERVE ½ CUP PAN JUICES FOR FILLING.
2	TBSPS. OIL
¼	CUP MINCED ONION
¼	CUP FINELY CHOPPED CELERY
¼	CUP FINELY CHOPPED CARROT
2	TBSPS. MINCED PARSLEY
¾	TSP. SALT
¼	TSP. OREGANO
¼	TSP. BASIL
⅛	TSP. NUTMEG
½	TSP. WHITE PEPPER
1	CUP RICOTTA OR CREAMED COTTAGE CHEESE
2	EGG YOLKS
½	CUP FRESH GROUND PARMESAN CHEESE
½	CUP CHICKEN BROTH

THIS RECIPE CONTINUED 115.

VOLUNTEER WORKERS ARE GOOD FOR NOTHING!

CANNELLONI

CONTINUED FROM PAGE 114

CHEDDAR SAUCE

4	TBSPS. MELTED BUTTER
5	TBSPS. FLOUR
1	10 oz. CAN CHICKEN BROTH
	SALT AND PEPPER TO TASTE
1	CUP GRATED CHEDDAR CHEESE
1	CUP MINDLESS MEAT SAUCE, PAGE 117
1/2	CUP LIGHT CREAM
1	PKG. KNORR'S SWISS HOLLANDAISE
	SAUCE OR YOUR OWN RECIPE
3	6 oz. PKGS. MONTEREY JACK CHEESE
20	CANNELLONI SHELLS, OR....
	20 CREPES (SEE "BEST OF BRIDGE")

CHICKEN FILLING

COOK CHICKEN AND FINELY CHOP OR GRIND MEAT. COMBINE OIL, ONION, CELERY, CARROTS AND PARSLEY IN SAUCEPAN AND COOK FOR 10 MINUTES. BEAT EGG YOLKS IN LARGE BOWL, ADD PARMESAN CHEESE AND RICOTTA OR COTTAGE CHEESE AND BEAT UNTIL SMOOTH. ADD SALT, OREGANO, BASIL, NUTMEG AND PEPPER. ADD CHICKEN, PAN JUICE, CHICKEN BROTH. BEAT UNTIL WELL MIXED. THIS MAY BE COVERED AND REFRIGERATED OR FROZEN UNTIL READY TO USE.

THIS RECIPE CONTINUED PAGE 116.

CANNELLONI

CONTINUED FROM PAGE 115.

CHEDDAR SAUCE

MELT BUTTER IN SAUCE PAN, ADD FLOUR UNTIL SMOOTH, THEN CAREFULLY ADD CHICKEN BROTH, STIRRING CONSTANTLY. ADD SALT AND PEPPER TO TASTE. STIR IN CHEDDAR CHEESE UNTIL WELL BLENDED AND THICK. NOW ADD PREPARED MEAT SAUCE AND CREAM. (SEE PAGE 117 FOR MINDLESS MEAT SAUCE.)

HOLLANDAISE SAUCE

PREPARE YOUR OWN OR COOK ACCORDING TO PACKAGE INSTRUCTIONS. ADD TO CHEDDAR SAUCE.

COOK CANNELLONI SHELLS IN BOILING, SALTED WATER FOR 8 MINUTES, DRAIN AND RINSE IN COLD WATER, OR HAVE CREPES PREPARED. DON'T BE CONCERNED IF SHELLS SPLIT. IT MAKES THEM EASIER TO FILL.

SPOON THIN LAYER OF SAUCE IN TWO 9"×13" PANS. USING APPROXIMATELY 2 TBSPS. CHICKEN FILLING PER SHELL, SHAPE FILLING IN HANDS AND INSERT IN SHELL OR ROLL UP IN SHELL OR CREPE. PLACE IN PANS, SIDE BY SIDE, WITH 5 IN EACH ROW. CAREFULLY SPOON SAUCE AROUND CANNELLONI.

CONTINUED ON PAGE 117.

CANNELLONI

Continued from page 116.
Cover each cannelloni completely with strips of Monterey Jack cheese. You really can't use too much. Bake in preheated 425° oven for 10 minutes, until cheese is bubbling. Serve at once.

If you're making the entire recipe in advance, prepare to the baking stage and freeze. As this is a rich meal, serve with a green salad and rolls.

MINDLESS MEAT SAUCE

Mindless, because of its simplicity.

1½	lbs. lean ground beef
¼	tsp. sage
¼	tsp. oregano
1	tbsp. salt
½	tsp. pepper
1	medium onion, finely chopped
15	large mushrooms, finely chopped
3	cloves garlic, minced
1	28 oz. can tomatoes, chopped, with juice
1	10 oz. can tomato sauce
1	5½ oz. can tomato paste

This recipe continued page 118.

MINDLESS MEAT SAUCE

CONTINUED FROM PAGE 117.

PREHEAT OVEN TO 350°. IN LARGE ROASTING PAN, SPREAD GROUND BEEF. COOK FOR 30 MINUTES, STIRRING OCCASIONALLY TO SEPARATE. MEANWHILE, COMBINE SAGE, OREGANO, SALT, PEPPER, ONION, MUSHROOMS AND GARLIC IN SAUCEPAN AND COOK AT MEDIUM HEAT UNTIL ONIONS ARE TRANSPARENT. SPREAD OVER MEAT AND CONTINUE COOKING IN OVEN FOR 15 MINUTES MORE. REMOVE FROM OVEN AND ADD CANNED TOMATOES, TOMATO SAUCE AND PASTE. BRING TO BOIL, THEN SIMMER FOR 1 HOUR OR LONGER. ADD SALT TO TASTE. STORE IN CONTAINERS AND FREEZE. USE IT IN ANY RECIPE CALLING FOR MEAT SAUCE, SUCH AS SPAGHETTI, LASAGNE, OR CANNELLONI.

AN AFTER DINNER MINT IS WHAT A MAN NEEDS TO PAY FOR THE RESTAURANT CHECK.

SUPER FOR ANY BUFFET OR CROWD !! (SEE PICTURE).

10 to 12	LB. HAM; WHOLE, FULLY COOKED
1½	CUPS COARSELY CHOPPED DRIED APRICOTS
1	CUP FINELY CHOPPED PECANS
8½	OZ. CAN CRUSHED PINEAPPLE, UNDRAINED
¼	TSP. THYME
1	12 OZ. CAN APRICOT NECTAR
½	TSP. GROUND ALLSPICE
½	CUP HONEY

HAVE THE BUTCHER REMOVE BONE FROM HAM. GRIND UP ½ LB. LEAN HAM FROM CAVITY. IN A LARGE BOWL COMBINE GROUND HAM WITH DRIED APRICOTS, PECANS, PINEAPPLE AND THYME. MIX WELL. SPOON INTO CAVITY. COVER END WITH FOIL AND HOLD WITH SKEWERS. (I ALWAYS SEEM TO HAVE TOO MUCH FOR THE CAVITY SO I COOK AND COVER THE REMAINDER IN A CASSEROLE ON THE SIDE.) POUR APRICOT NECTAR OVER HAM, SPRINKLE WITH ALLSPICE. COVER ROASTING PAN WITH FOIL. BAKE 2 HOURS AT 325°. REMOVE FROM OVEN AND SPREAD HALF THE HONEY OVER HAM. BAKE, UNCOVERED 30 MINUTES; BRUSH WITH REMAINING HONEY AND BAKE 15 MINUTES LONGER. SERVES 16-20.

FAILURE MAY BE YOUR THING.

BONES

Most butcher shops now sell the rib bones cut from the prime or standing rib-roasts. A treat! Serve 2 per person.

Rib Bones
Garlic salt and seasoned pepper,
(lots of both)
2 tbsps. dry mustard
3 tbsps. cream
Bread crumbs
3 tbsps. butter, melted

Preheat broiler. Generously sprinkle bones with garlic salt and seasoned pepper. Make a paste of mustard and cream. Brush each rib with paste and sprinkle each with fine bread crumbs. Place ribs on broiler pan and broil three minutes per side, brushing with melted butter while turning, 10 to 12 minutes in total or until well browned and crispy. Serve with baked potatoes and vegetables. Really delicious.

If you really look like your passport photo, chances are you're not well enough to travel.

Chicken 'N Noodle
Casserole Extraordinaire

This is a quick luncheon or dinner dish. Prepare in the morning and refrigerate until cooking time. Serve with a tossed salad and a jellied salad and dinner rolls. Serves 12 to 14.

1	10 oz. pkg. uncooked wide noodles
4	5 oz. cans boned chicken or....
	2 full cups cooked chicken
1	10 oz. can condensed cream of
	mushroom soup
1	10 oz. can condensed cream of
	celery soup
1	10 oz. can condensed cream of
	chicken soup
1	4½ oz. can chopped ripe olives
1	10 oz. can mushrooms, drained
½	cup wine or sherry
1	lb. cheddar cheese, grated
	paprika

Cook noodles; drain. Mix remaining ingredients with noodles except cheese. Spoon into a shallow 9"x13" baking dish. Top with grated cheese. Sprinkle with paprika. Bake at 350° for 20 to 25 minutes. Cheese should be melted. If you refrigerate this casserole beforehand, let it stand at room temperature at least 1 hour before baking.

Coquille David

David serves this delectable dish to the tender, sweet, young things that drop over for dinner. A leafy green salad, a bottle of wine, soft music and thou — it's a sure thing! Serves 6 as an appetizer or 4 as a main course. (Pictured on cover.)

1	lb. scallops
½	lb. fresh mushrooms, sliced
1	cup dry white wine or....
	3/4 cup dry vermouth
½	tsp. salt
4	peppercorns
2	slices of onion
1	bay leaf
¼	tsp. thyme

Sauce

3	tbsps. butter
4	tbsps. flour
3/4	cup milk
2	egg yolks
½	cup whipping cream
	pinch of cayenne
	salt to taste
2	tbsps. dry sherry or brandy
½	cup swiss cheese, grated

This recipe continued page 123.

COQUILLE DAVID

CONTINUED FROM PAGE 122

RINSE SCALLOPS IN COLD WATER. COMBINE SCALLOPS AND MUSHROOMS IN A SAUCEPAN WITH NEXT SIX INGREDIENTS AND ENOUGH WATER TO BARELY COVER. BRING TO BOIL, COVER AND SIMMER GENTLY FOR 5 MINUTES. REMOVE SCALLOPS AND MUSHROOMS. STRAIN LIQUID AND BOIL RAPIDLY UNTIL REDUCED TO 1 CUP. REMOVE SCALLOPS AND CUT INTO SMALL PIECES.

<u>SAUCE</u> - IN A DOUBLE BOILER, MELT BUTTER AND STIR IN FLOUR. SLOWLY ADD HOT SCALLOP LIQUID AND MILK, STIRRING CONSTANTLY, UNTIL THICK. MIX EGG YOLKS AND CREAM TOGETHER, ADD SOME OF THE HOT SAUCE AND RETURN ALL TO SAUCEPAN. COOK OVER LOW HEAT FOR APPROXIMATELY 5 MINUTES. SEASON TO TASTE WITH SALT AND CAYENNE. FOLD IN SHERRY, MUSHROOMS AND SCALLOPS. SPOON INTO BUTTERED SCALLOP SHELLS (FOR APPETIZERS) OR ONION SOUP BOWLS (FOR MAIN COURSE), AND SPRINKLE WITH SWISS CHEESE. BAKE AT 375° UNTIL LIGHT BROWN AND BUBBLY - ABOUT 15 MINUTES.

<u>NOTE</u>: ½ CUP BUTTERED BREAD CRUMBS MAY BE SPRINKLED OVER THE CHEESE BEFORE BAKING IF DESIRED. THIS MAY BE MADE AHEAD AND REFRIGERATED BEFORE BAKING.

CRAB STUFFED CHICKEN BREASTS
(SEE PICTURE, COVER)

6   WHOLE CHICKEN BREASTS,
        BONED AND SKINNED

STUFFING

- ½   CUP HERB-SEASONED STUFFING MIX, (MRS. MCCUBBISON'S)
- 1   5 OZ. CAN CRABMEAT, DRAINED AND FLAKED
- ½   CUP CHOPPED CELERY
- ½   CUP CHOPPED GREEN ONION
- 3   TBSPS. BUTTER
- 3   TBSPS. DRY WHITE WINE
-     PAPRIKA

SAUCE

- ⅓   CUP KRAFT SWISS CHEESE, GRATED
- ⅓   CUP DRY WHITE WINE
- 3   TBSPS. BUTTER
- 3   TBSPS. FLOUR
- 1   PINT HALF & HALF CREAM

PREPARE STUFFING – PLACE BUTTER IN A MIXING BOWL AND MELT IN MICROWAVE FOR 30 SECONDS. ADD ONION AND CELERY AND COOK 2 MINUTES, UNCOVERED, STIRRING ONCE. ADD WINE, STUFFING MIX AND CRABMEAT. MIX WELL. SET ASIDE.

THIS RECIPE CONTINUED PAGE 125.

CRAB-STUFFED CHICKEN BREASTS

CONTINUED FROM PAGE 124.

POUND CHICKEN TO FLATTEN BY PLACING BETWEEN 2 SHEETS OF WAX PAPER AND POUND WITH A ROLLING PIN, UNTIL QUITE THIN AND UNIFORM. SPRINKLE WITH SALT AND PEPPER. DIVIDE STUFFING MIXTURE AMONG BREASTS, ROLL UP AND SECURE WITH TOOTH PICKS. SPRINKLE WITH PAPRIKA. COVER WITH WAXED PAPER AND COOK IN MICROWAVE OVEN 10 MINUTES, TURNING DISH ONCE.

NOTE: FOR CONVENTIONAL OVEN— MELT BUTTER AND COOK INGREDIENTS FOR STUFFING IN SAUCE- PAN OVER MEDIUM HEAT. BAKE CHICKEN, COVERED, AT 375° FOR 45 MINUTES. SERVES 6.

<u>PREPARE SAUCE</u> — MELT BUTTER IN SAUCEPAN, ADD FLOUR, STIR UNTIL WELL MIXED. GRADUALLY ADD CREAM AND COOK, STIRRING CONSTANTLY, UNTIL SMOOTH. ADD WINE AND CHEESE AND CONTINUE COOKING UNTIL CHEESE IS MELTED. WHEN READY TO SERVE, REMOVE TOOTH PICKS FROM CHICKEN AND POUR SAUCE OVER.

THEY SAY SMOKING SHORTENS YOUR LIFE. IT ALSO SHORTENS YOUR CIGARETTES.

Eureka! Enchiladas

½	cup olive oil
2	cloves garlic (as much as you can stand), minced
1	14 oz. can dark pitted olives (reserve juice)
1	10 oz. can tomato sauce
1	10 oz. can water
2	rounded tbsps. chili powder
1	tsp. cumin
2	tsps. salt
2	large onions, diced
1	lb. Monterey Jack cheese
1	lb. lean ground beef
1½	doz. tortillas (frozen are best)

Sauce

Sauté minced garlic in olive oil. Add olive juice, tomato sauce, water, chili powder, cumin and salt. Simmer 10 minutes.

Filling

Sauté diced onions, diced olives and ground beef in 1 tbsp. olive oil until onions are transparent. Add ¾ lb. grated cheese, remove from heat and allow cheese to melt through the filling mixture.

For tortillas see next page.

Eureka-Enchiladas

Continued from page 126.

Tortillas

Fry tortillas one at a time in 3 tbsps. olive oil at high temperature, turning once. Remove from heat. Dry between paper towels. Spread with small amount of sauce. Place 1 heaping tbsp. of filling on each tortilla. Roll up like a crêpe and lay in a rectangular oven dish. Add remaining sauce. Sprinkle remaining filling and remaining 1/4 lb. grated cheese over the rolled tortillas.

Bake at 350° for 30 minutes. Serves 8.

"Are you married?"
"No, I was hit by a car."

La Corneille Ivre

Preheat oven to 450°.
Place small amount of garlic flavored butter in bottom of roasting pan. Stuff and truss one medium sized crow. Roast between 2 rocks for 6 hours. When you can put a fork through the rock, the crow is done.

The Gaffer's Spaghetti Sauce

1	LB. LEAN GROUND BEEF
1	ONION, FINELY CHOPPED
1	10 oz. CAN BUTTON MUSHROOMS, RESERVE LIQUID
	SALT, PEPPER AND GARLIC SALT, TO TASTE
1	14 oz. CAN TOMATO SAUCE
1	28 oz. CAN TOMATOES, CUT UP
3/4	CUP CHILI SAUCE, (SEE "BEST OF BRIDGE")
1/4 to 1/2	TSP. EACH; OREGANO, MARJORAM, THYME (ANY OR ALL, AS YOU WISH)
1/4	CUP DRY RED WINE

SAUTÉ BEEF, ONION, MUSHROOMS, SALT, PEPPER AND GARLIC SALT, CRUMBLING MEAT AS FINELY AS POSSIBLE UNTIL BROWNED. IF YOUR MEAT IS NOT LEAN, BE SURE TO DRAIN ANY EXCESS FAT. ADD MUSHROOM LIQUID, TOMATO SAUCE, TOMATOES, CHILI SAUCE, OREGANO, MARJORAM, THYME AND SALT TO TASTE. IF YOU DON'T HAVE THE CHILI SAUCE MADE UP, SUBSTITUTE 1 TBSP. BROWN SUGAR, 2 TBSPS. KETCHUP AND 1 RED CHILI PEPPER, CRUSHED. COOK OVER LOW HEAT ONE HOUR UNTIL ALL INGREDIENTS GET TO KNOW EACH OTHER. SOME WATER MAY BE ADDED AS THIS THICKENS. DON'T BE AFRAID TO PLAY WITH THE SPICES A BIT TO SUIT YOUR OWN TASTE. ADD THE RED WINE BEFORE SERVING. SERVES 8.

PICTURED ON OVERLEAF:

SUPPER CASSEROLES

SATÉ
     PAGE 129
MANDARIN ORANGE SALAD
     PAGE 71

SATÉ

RAVE NOTICES: A BAR-B-QUED INDONESIAN DISH WE HIGHLY RECOMMEND FOR YOUR NEXT DINNER PARTY OR SUMMER COOKOUT. THERE WON'T BE A SPECK LEFT OVER. (SEE PICTURE).

1½	LBS. PORK TENDERLOIN
¼	CUP BUTTER
1	TBSP. LEMON JUICE
	GRATED LEMON RIND
½	TSP. TABASCO
3	TBSPS. GRATED ONION
3	TSPS. BROWN SUGAR
1	TSP. CORIANDER
½	TSP. GROUND CUMIN
¼	TSP. GINGER
1	CLOVE GARLIC, CRUSHED
½	CUP INDONESIAN SOYA SAUCE
	(BRAND NAME: CONIMEX, KETJAP BENTANG MANIS - SWEET - TRY A EUROPEAN DELICATESSAN) OR... SUBSTITUTE KIKOMAN TERIYAKI SAUCE.
	SALT AND PEPPER TO TASTE (DON'T OVERSALT)
	SMALL 8" WOODEN SKEWERS.

THIS RECIPE CONTINUED 130.

DEFINITION OF A PICNIC: MEADOW LARK.

SATÉ

CONTINUED FROM PAGE 129.

CUT PORK TENDERLOIN INTO 3/4" CUBES AND PLACE IN SHALLOW DISH. MELT BUTTER IN SAUCEPAN AND ADD REMAINING INGREDIENTS. BRING TO A BOIL AND SIMMER 5 MINUTES. POUR OVER MEAT, COVER AND LEAVE OVERNIGHT IN FRIG. TURN THE MEAT PERIODICALLY (BUTTER WILL CONGEAL BUT DON'T WORRY). REMOVE MEAT FROM MARINADE (RESERVE) AND PUT 5 OR 6 PIECES ON EACH SKEWER. GRILL ON BAR-B-QUE FOR 15 MINUTES OR UNTIL DONE (DON'T OVERCOOK). TURN FREQUENTLY - WILL KEEP IN A WARM OVEN TILL DINNER IS SERVED - BUT BEST STRAIGHT OFF THE GRILL. REHEAT MARINADE AND POUR OVER MEAT. SET ON A PLATTER IN A BED OF RICE. GREAT WITH SPINACH SALAD. SERVES 6 TO 8.

PEACHY PORK

4	PORK STEAKS - FAT REMOVED
1	TBSP. OIL
1	TSP. BASIL, SALT & PEPPER TO TASTE
1	28 OZ. CAN PEACH SLICES
1	TBSP. VINEGAR
2	BEEF BOUILLON CUBES, CRUSHED

THIS RECIPE CONTINUED PAGE 131.

Peachy Pork

Continued from page 130.
Heat oil in skillet. Add meat and brown. Drain. Drain peach syrup and add to it; basil, salt, pepper, vinegar and crushed beef cubes. Combine meat and peach syrup mixture in skillet. Cover and simmer 30 minutes. Add water if necessary. 5 minutes before serving, add peaches. Heat through. Serve with buttered rice. Serves 4.

Goulash

2	lbs. Hamburger
2	pkgs. Kraft Dinner
1	cup celery, sliced
1	onion, chopped
2	10 oz. cans mushrooms
1	tbsp. HP sauce
	dash Tabasco
4	10 oz. cans tomato soup
1	large green pepper, sliced
2	10 oz. cans mushroom soup
1	10 oz. can Niblets corn
1	tbsp. Worcestershire sauce
1	tbsp. curry powder (optional)

Brown hamburger and onion. Drain off excess fat. Cook Kraft dinner. Combine everything, including cheese from Kraft dinner. Bake at 325° for one hour. Serves 10.

Sweet 'n Sour Chili Ribs

The aroma of these ribs will bring your family running. A great dinner to prepare at noon, place in the oven and forget. Serve with rice and a green salad.

4	lbs. lean pork spare ribs
3/4	cup brown sugar
1/2	cup ketchup
1/2	cup white vinegar
2	tbsps. Worcestershire sauce
1	tsp. chili powder
3/4	cup water
1	onion, diced

Trim fat off ribs and cut in desired sizes. Spread in bottom of large, shallow baking dish or roaster. Mix all other ingredients in medium sized bowl. Pour over ribs and bake uncovered at 250° for 3 hours. Serves 4 to 6.

We really don't need any calendars. When it rains, it's Sunday.

Cantonese Chicken

- 1 CAN PINEAPPLE TIDBITS
- 1 CUP SLICED CELERY
- 1 CUP THINLY SLICED CARROTS
- 1/4 CUP CHOPPED ONIONS
- 1/4 CUP TOASTED SLIVERED ALMONDS
- 1/4 CUP BUTTER
- 1 TBSP. ARROWROOT OR CORNSTARCH
- 1/4 TSP. GINGER - 1/8 TSP. NUTMEG
- 3/4 CUP WATER
- 1 TBSP. SOYA SAUCE
- 1 TSP. LEMON JUICE
- 1 TSP. CHICKEN SEASONED STOCK BASE
- 1 1/2 CUPS CHOPPED, COOKED CHICKEN
- 1 5 OZ. CAN WATER CHESTNUTS, DRAINED AND SLICED THIN
- CHOW MEIN NOODLES OR RICE

DRAIN PINEAPPLE; RESERVE JUICE. SAUTÉ CELERY, CARROTS, ONIONS AND ALMONDS IN BUTTER IN LARGE SKILLET UNTIL ONIONS ARE GOLDEN BROWN. COMBINE ARROWROOT, GINGER, NUTMEG, PINEAPPLE JUICE, WATER, SOYA SAUCE, LEMON JUICE AND SEASONED STOCK BASE, MIXING UNTIL WELL BLENDED. ADD TO SAUTÉED VEGETABLES AND COOK UNTIL MIXTURE THICKENS, STIRRING CONSTANTLY. STIR IN PINEAPPLE TIDBITS, CHICKEN AND WATER CHESTNUTS. COVER AND SIMMER 10 TO 15 MINUTES. SERVE OVER CHOW MEIN NOODLES OR RICE. SERVES 4.

CHOP SUEY

THIS IS A YUMMY WAY TO USE UP LEFT-OVERS. SERVED WITH RICE AND A SWEET DISH, SUCH AS JAPANESE CHICKEN WINGS OR ORIENTAL MEATBALLS ("THE BEST OF BRIDGE") IT MAKES A REAL FEED OF CHINESE COOKING. SERVE WITH ADDITIONAL SOYA SAUCE. SERVES 6 TO 8.

2	CUPS LEFT-OVER ROAST PORK, BEEF OR CHICKEN
3	TBSPS. SOYA SAUCE
1	TBSP. BROWN SUGAR
4	TBSPS. SALAD OIL
3	MEDIUM ONIONS, SLICED
2	CLOVES GARLIC, MINCED
1	GREEN PEPPER, CUT IN STRIPS
2	CUPS SLICED CELERY
1	CUP WATER
1	CUP SLICED MUSHROOMS, FRESH OR CANNED AND DRAINED
2	TBSPS. CORNSTARCH
1/2	TSP. SALT
3/4	TSP. SEASONED SALT
1/4	TSP. PEPPER
1	19 oz. CAN BEAN SPROUTS, DRAINED AND RINSED OR....
2	CUPS. FRESH BEAN SPROUTS

THIS RECIPE CONTINUED PAGE 135.

CHOP SUEY

CONTINUED FROM PAGE 134.

SLICE ALL VEGETABLES. SLICE MEAT THINLY, REMOVING EXCESS FAT. COMBINE SOYA SAUCE, BROWN SUGAR AND MIX WITH MEAT. STIR AND LET STAND FOR 15 MINUTES. IN SKILLET OR WOK, HEAT OIL AND ADD ONION AND GARLIC. SAUTÉ FOR 2 OR 3 MINUTES ON LOW HEAT AND ADD MEAT AND SOYA MARINADE. STIR, COVER AND COOK 5 MINUTES ON MEDIUM HEAT. ADD VEGETABLES AND STIR TOGETHER. ADD WATER MIXED WITH CORNSTARCH, SALTS AND PEPPER. ADD BEAN SPROUTS, STIR AND COVER. COOK 5 MINUTES.

THE MOON NOT ONLY PULLS THE OCEANS BACK AND FORTH IN THE TIDES, IT STOPS CARS ON THE SIDES OF THE ROADS.

GINGER'S BEEF STROGANOFF

GREAT FOR LARGE CROWDS (ADJUST RECIPE ACCORDINGLY). FREEZES BEAUTIFULLY — BUT DON'T ADD SOUR CREAM AND SHERRY UNTIL DAY OF SERVING. SERVES 4 TO 6.

1	LB. BEEF SIRLOIN, CUT AGAINST GRAIN INTO 1/4" x 1" PIECES
2	TBSPS. BUTTER
1	CUP SLICED FRESH MUSHROOMS
1/2	CUP CHOPPED ONION
1	GARLIC CLOVE, MINCED
3	TBSPS. FLOUR
3	TBSPS. BUTTER
1	TBSP. TOMATO PASTE
1	10 OZ. CAN BEEF BOUILLON
1/2	TSP. SALT
1	CUP SOUR CREAM
2	TBSPS. SHERRY

BROWN MEAT QUICKLY IN A HOT SKILLET. REMOVE TO CASSEROLE DISH. REDUCE SKILLET HEAT AND ADD MUSHROOMS, ONIONS AND GARLIC (ADD MORE BUTTER IF NECESSARY). COOK 3 TO 4 MINUTES UNTIL ONION IS CLEAR. REMOVE AND ADD TO THE CASSEROLE DISH. NOW MAKE THE SAUCE IN THE SKILLET. MELT BUTTER, ADD FLOUR, SALT AND TOMATO PASTE. STIR IN BEEF BOUILLON AND COOK UNTIL THICK. ADD SAUCE TO CASSEROLE.

TO SERVE, SEE NEXT PAGE!

Ginger's Beef Stroganoff

Continued from page 136.
When ready to serve add sour cream and sherry to casserole and heat in 275° oven for ½ hour or until warmed through. <u>Don't</u> let it boil or sour cream will curdle.

Fandango

1   lb. ground beef
1   medium onion, chopped
1   10 oz. can mushrooms, drained
1 or 2 garlic cloves, crushed
1   tsp. oregano
1 or 2 - 10 oz. pkgs. chopped spinach,
       thawed and drained
1   10 oz. can cream of celery soup
1   cup sour cream
1   tbsp. uncooked minute rice
    salt and pepper
1   6 oz. pkg. mozzarella cheese

Brown meat, onions, mushrooms, garlic and oregano in a frying pan. Stir in spinach, soup, sour cream, rice and salt and pepper to taste. Place cheese (grated or cut in strips) on top. Bake in 350° oven for 35 to 45 minutes. If you are a cheese fan, double the amount called for and layer this in the middle of the casserole. Serves 6.

DIVINE CHICKEN DIVAN

THIS IS ALSO A GOOD WAY TO USE LEFT-OVER SLICES OF TURKEY BREAST. SERVES 10.

5	WHOLE CHICKEN BREASTS, SPLIT
1	LARGE BUNCH OF BROCCOLI (FRESH)
½	CUP BUTTER
½	CUP FLOUR
4	CUPS CHICKEN STOCK
3	EGG YOLKS
1	CUP WHIPPING CREAM, WHIPPED
6	TBSPS. SHERRY
	SALT AND PEPPER TO TASTE
½	CUP GRATED PARMESAN CHEESE – (OR MORE IF YOU LIKE)

COOK OR GENTLY SAUTÉ CHICKEN BREASTS UNTIL TENDER. REMOVE AND DEBONE. COOK THE BROCCOLI AND SEASON LIGHTLY, DRAIN AND SET ASIDE. MELT BUTTER, STIR IN FLOUR AND THEN ADD THE CHICKEN STOCK. COOK, STIRRING CONSTANTLY, UNTIL MIXTURE COMES TO A BOIL. SIMMER GENTLY FOR ABOUT 5 MINUTES. COOL SLIGHTLY, THEN BEAT IN THE EGG YOLKS. WHIP THE CREAM (NOT TOO STIFF) AND FOLD IT IN WITH THE SHERRY. PLACE THE BROCCOLI IN THE BOTTOM OF AN OVEN PROOF DISH. COVER BROCCOLI WITH HALF THE SAUCE AND COVER WITH GRATED CHEESE.

THIS RECIPE CONTINUED PAGE 139.

Divine Chicken Divan

CONTINUED FROM PAGE 138.

ARRANGE THE CHICKEN OVER THE CHEESE COVERED BROCCOLI AND TOP WITH THE REMAINING SAUCE AND ADDITIONAL CHEESE IF DESIRED. BAKE AT 350° FOR 20 MINUTES — JUST UNTIL VERY HOT. IF DESIRED YOU CAN PUT UNDER THE BROILER FOR A MINUTE TO BROWN AT THE VERY END OF THE HEATING PERIOD. THIS DISH CAN BE MADE AHEAD AS IT FREEZES WELL.

Barbequed Chicken Marinade

½ CUP SOYA SAUCE
¼ CUP SHERRY
½ CUP COOKING OIL
JUICE OF ONE ORANGE
GRATED ORANGE RIND
FRESHLY GRATED BLACK PEPPER
2 CLOVES GARLIC, CHOPPED
FRESHLY GRATED GINGER ROOT
½ CUP HONEY

MARINATE CHICKEN HALVES OR PIECES FOR SEVERAL HOURS OR OVERNIGHT, TURNING FREQUENTLY. ARRANGE CHICKEN IN SPIT BASKET (SKIN SIDE OUT) AND TURN MOTOR ON. COOK OVER COALS 1½ HOURS. DURING LAST ½ HOUR BASTE WITH MARINADE TO WHICH ½ CUP HONEY HAS BEEN ADDED.

Stroganoff Meatballs

THIS CASSEROLE CAN BE MADE AHEAD AND KEPT IN THE REFRIGERATOR. SERVE IT WITH BROAD EGG NOODLES AND A GREEN VEGETABLE.

Meat Balls

2	LBS. GROUND BEEF
1½	CUPS BREAD CRUMBS
¼	CUP MILK
¼	CUP CHOPPED ONION
2	EGGS, BEATEN
1	TSP. SALT
	PEPPER TO TASTE

Sauce

½	CUP CHOPPED ONION
4	TBSPS. BUTTER
2	TBSPS. FLOUR
2	TBSPS. KETCHUP
1	10 OZ. CAN CONSOMMÉ (UNDILUTED)
1	CUP SOUR CREAM

MEAT BALLS - COMBINE ALL INGREDIENTS IN LARGE BOWL. MIX WELL AND ROLL INTO BALLS OF DESIRED SIZE. PLACE ON EDGED COOKIE SHEET AND BAKE AT 375° FOR 25 TO 30 MINUTES. REMOVE FROM OVEN, DRAIN AND SET ASIDE.

FOR SAUCE, SEE PAGE 141.

STROGANOFF MEATBALLS

CONTINUED FROM PAGE 140.

SAUCE - BROWN ONION IN BUTTER, ADD FLOUR, MIX WELL. ADD KETCHUP AND CONSOMMÉ, COOKING SLOWLY UNTIL THICKENED. ADD SOUR CREAM, THEN MEAT BALLS. PLACE IN CASSEROLE AND HEAT IN 300° OVEN UNTIL SERVING TIME.

HAM CASSEROLE

A TASTY WAY TO USE THAT LEFT-OVER HAM. SERVES 6.

1	CUP CUBED COOKED POTATOES
½	CUP CHOPPED ONIONS
2	TBSPS. BUTTER
3	TBSPS. FLOUR
½	TSP. SALT AND PEPPER TO TASTE
1¼	CUPS MILK
½	CUP SHREDDED SWISS CHEESE
2	CUPS CUBED COOKED HAM (OR MORE)
1½	CUPS SOFT BREAD CRUMBS
2	TBSPS. BUTTER

COOK ONIONS IN BUTTER IN SKILLET, BLEND IN FLOUR, SALT AND PEPPER. ADD MILK SLOWLY. COOK UNTIL THICK. ADD CHEESE AND MELT. ADD HAM AND POTATOES - MIX AND POUR INTO YOUR FAVORITE CASSEROLE DISH. SPRINKLE WITH BREAD CRUMBS AND DOT WITH 2 TBSPS. OF BUTTER. COOK AT 400° FOR 30 MINUTES.

Veal Scallopini

Italian in origin, this famous recipe is party fare. Serves 6.

1½	LBS. VEAL STEAK (½" THICK)
1	TSP. SALT
1	TSP. PAPRIKA
½	CUP SALAD OIL
¼	CUP LEMON JUICE
1	CLOVE GARLIC (SPLIT)
1	TSP. PREPARED MUSTARD
¼	TSP. NUTMEG
½	TSP. SUGAR
¼	CUP FLOUR
¼	CUP OIL
1	MEDIUM ONION, SLICED THIN
1	GREEN PEPPER CUT IN STRIPS
1	10 OZ. CAN CHICKEN BROTH
¼	LB. MUSHROOMS, SLICED
1	TBSP. BUTTER
6	PIMENTO OLIVES, SLICED

Sauce

Combine salt, paprika, oil, lemon juice, garlic, mustard, nutmeg and sugar in a jar. Shake to combine thoroughly.

This recipe continued page 143.

Veal Scallopini

Continued from page 142.

Cut veal into serving pieces. Spread veal in shallow dish - pour sauce over - coat well and let stand 20 minutes. Remove garlic. Heat oil in large skillet. Lift veal from sauce and dip in flour. Brown in skillet and add onion and green pepper. Combine chicken broth with remaining sauce and pour over veal. Continue cooking slowly (covered) until veal is tender. (About 30 minutes.) Brown mushrooms lightly in butter. Add mushrooms and olives to veal. Serve on large platter surrounded with noodles and garnish with parsley and lemon wedges.

A lot of women don't care who wears the pants in the family, as long as there is money in the pockets.

Sweet & Sour Spare Ribs

Absolutely Excellent!

3 to 4 lbs. Pork Spare Ribs
   (Pork Button Bones are also good;
   Bite Sized and Meaty)
1/4   cup Vinegar
3   tbsps. Soya Sauce
1   tsp. Sugar
1/2   tsp. Pepper
4   tbsps. Flour
2   tbsps. Cooking Oil

Sweet & Sour Sauce
1/2   cup Vinegar
1 1/2   cups Brown Sugar
1   cup Water
1   tbsp. Cornstarch dissolved in....
1/4   cup Water

Optional
1   14oz. tin Pineapple Tidbits
   Replace 1/2 cup Water with....
1/2   cup Pineapple Juice

This recipe continued page 145.

Gardening didn't keep Adam out of Mischief

PICTURED ON OVERLEAF:

SUPPER CASSEROLE

SCAMPI
    PAGE 102

SWEET & SOUR SPARE RIBS

CONTINUED FROM PAGE 144.

CUT RIBS INTO SERVING-SIZE PIECES AND PLACE IN LARGE POT. COVER WITH WATER AND ADD VINEGAR. BRING TO BOIL AND SIMMER 1 HOUR. DRAIN. MAKE MARINADE OF SOYA SAUCE, SUGAR AND PEPPER. POUR OVER RIBS (USE SAME POT) AND TURN FREQUENTLY TO COVER EACH PIECE. REMOVE RIBS AND SHAKE IN BROWN PAPER BAG WITH FLOUR. IN A LARGE SKILLET, ADD COOKING OIL AND BROWN RIBS (NOT TOO LONG OR THEY'LL DRY OUT). PLACE IN LARGE CASSEROLE DISH. IN A SAUCEPAN, COMBINE SAUCE INGREDIENTS AND COOK OVER MEDIUM HEAT UNTIL SLIGHTLY THICK. (IF USING PINEAPPLE, PLACE TIDBITS IN CASSEROLE WITH RIBS.) POUR OVER RIBS AND SET IN 350° OVEN FOR AT LEAST ½ HOUR. FLOUR ON RIBS WILL THICKEN THE SAUCE. SERVE OVER A BED OF RICE.

AFTER PAYING FOR THE WEDDING, ABOUT ALL A FATHER HAS LEFT TO GIVE AWAY IS THE BRIDE.

ROAST DUCK WITH PAT'S ORANGE SAUCE

2   DUCKS, WILD OR DOMESTIC
1   CARROT
2   STALKS CELERY
1   LARGE ONION
1   CUP DRY WHITE WINE
1   CUP WATER

SOAK CLEANED DUCKS FOR ½ HOUR IN BAKING SODA WATER (½ CUP BAKING SODA MIXED IN SINK OF COLD WATER). RINSE AND DRY CAVITIES AND OUTSIDES OF BIRDS WITH PAPER TOWELS. PLACE IN ROASTING PAN AND FILL CAVITIES AND SURROUND DUCKS WITH SLICES OF ONION, CARROT AND CELERY. (THESE WILL BE DISCARDED AFTER ROASTING.) COVER DUCKS WITH LAYER OF BUTTER. SPRINKLE GENEROUSLY WITH SALT AND PEPPER. POUR WHITE WINE AND 1 CUP WATER OVER DUCKS. COVER AND ROAST AT 350° FOR THE FIRST HOUR AND 300° FOR FINAL 3½ HOURS. (THIS IS THE SECRET FOR COOKING ANY WILD FOWL— SLOWLY AND FOR A LONG TIME.) MEAT WILL BE VERY TENDER AND LITERALLY FALL FROM THE CARCASS. YOU MAY WANT TO REMOVE THE MEAT FROM THE BONES AND SERVE IT IN THIS INFORMAL MANNER. SERVE WITH "PAT'S ORANGE SAUCE" WHICH CAN BE FOUND ON THE NEXT PAGE. THIS SERVES 4 – LOVE.

Pat's Special Orange Sauce

ESPECIALLY FOR ROAST DUCK.

1	10 OZ. CAN DRAINED MANDARIN ORANGE SECTIONS
4	TBSPS. BUTTER
4	TBSPS. FLOUR
2	TBSPS. "CHICKEN IN A MUG"
1	CUP HOT WATER
1	CUP ORANGE JUICE (MADE FROM UNSWEETENED FROZEN CONCENTRATE)
	DASH TABASCO
3/4	CUP CREAMED HONEY
	SHREDDED ORANGE PEEL

MELT BUTTER IN A SAUCEPAN, ADD FLOUR AND STIR UNTIL BUBBLY. MIX "CHICKEN IN A MUG", HOT WATER, ORANGE JUICE AND SHREDDED ORANGE PEEL. (USING POTATO PEELER, REMOVE PEEL FROM AN ORANGE AND CUT IN THIN JULIENNE STRIPS.) ADD TO BUTTER MIXTURE. STIR UNTIL THICKENED. ADD HONEY AND TABASCO. KEEP STIRRING AND ADD ORANGE SECTIONS. BEAT UNTIL FAIRLY SMOOTH AND SERVE HOT WITH DUCK.

"WHERE DOES VIRGIN WOOL COME FROM?"
"FROM SHEEP THAT RUN THE FASTEST."

Shellfish Puké

(That's "Poo-kay"). Serve with a green salad and rolls - you'll love it.

2	onions, sliced
4	cups water
1	small lemon, sliced
1½	tsps. salt
1	lb. scallops
1	lb. shrimp, shelled
½	lb. cooked crab meat, flaked
2	cups stale bread crumbs
2	cups milk
2	tbsps. butter
⅓	cup dry sherry
1	tsp. salt
½	tsp. white pepper
2 or 3	drops tabasco
⅓	lb. Monterey Jack cheese, thinly sliced
3	tbsps. Parmesan cheese
2	tbsps. butter, softened

Combine 4 cups water, one sliced onion, lemon and 1½ tsps. salt in a large saucepan and bring to a boil. Reduce heat to moderately low and add scallops. Poach for 2 or 3 minutes and transfer with a slotted spoon to a bowl. (Continued)

Shellfish Puke'

Continued from page 148.

After poaching, don't throw out liquid! Add shrimp to saucepan and simmer 3 minutes or until pink. Transfer them to a bowl. Reserve cooking liquid, discarding onion and lemon. Cut scallops into 1/4" slices. If large shrimp are used, cut them lengthwise. In a large bowl, combine shellfish with crabmeat.

Combine bread crumbs and milk in a saucepan and cook over moderate heat. Stir until it is the consistency of a paste. In a small saucepan cook second onion in 2 tbsps. butter over moderate heat, until softened. Add the onion mixture, sherry and enough of the reserved liquid to the paste to thin it to the consistency of sour cream. Season with 1 tsp. salt, white pepper and tabasco.

In buttered casserole arrange a layer of seafood, spread with a layer of paste and then Monterey Jack cheese. Continue to layer, ending with cheese. Sprinkle on parmesan and dot with softened butter. Preheat oven to 350° and bake for 30 minutes or until bubbling. (Cooking hint: when measuring sherry for cream sauce, measure some for the cook.) Serves 6.

ENGLISH SPICED BEEF

THIS IS TRADITIONAL CHRISTMAS FARE. PRODUCES A PINK AND HAMLIKE TEXTURE THAT, SLICED THINLY, IS A GREAT FAVORITE FOR HOLIDAY FEASTING. WELL WORTH THE TROUBLE!

PIECE OF LEAN BEEF, UP TO 25 LBS., DEBONED AND ROLLED

1½	OZ. SALTPETRE
1½	CUPS BROWN SUGAR
1¼	CUPS SALT
4	TBSPS. BLACK PEPPER
4	TBSPS. GROUND ALLSPICE
2	TBSPS. MACE
5	TSPS. NUTMEG
5	TSPS. CLOVES

MIX INGREDIENTS TOGETHER AND RUB ROUND OF BEEF. COVER LOOSELY WITH FOIL. SET IN A <u>COOL</u> PLACE (A CROCK POT IS IDEAL) AND TURN EVERY 2 OR 3 DAYS FOR 3 WEEKS. BEFORE BOILING, PUT A PIECE OF SUET IN WHERE BONE WAS TAKEN OUT. TIE FIRMLY WITH CORD UNTIL IT IS OF UNIFORM SHAPE. SIMMER GENTLY FOR 5 TO 7 HOURS TURNING AT HALF TIME. DO NOT WASH OFF SPICES BEFORE BOILING. FOR SMALLER PIECE OF BEEF (10 TO 12 LBS.) USE SAME AMOUNT OF SPICES BUT REDUCE PICKLING TIME TO 12 DAYS AND REDUCE BOILING TIME TO 3 TO 5 HOURS.

SHORT RIBS IN BEER

A PERENNIAL FAVORITE. MY RECIPE CARD IS COVERED WITH GREASE AND DULLED FROM YEARS OF USE.

8	SHORT RIBS (3 LBS. TRIMMED)
½	CUP FLOUR
¼	TSP. PEPPER
¼	TSP. GINGER
1	TSP. SALT
½	TSP. DRY MUSTARD
1	TSP. CHOPPED PARSLEY
2	TBSPS. OIL
1	MEDIUM ONION, SLICED
1	CLOVE GARLIC
12	OZ. BEER
5	CARROTS, SLICED

WASH AND DRY SHORT RIBS. COMBINE FLOUR, PEPPER, GINGER, SALT, DRY MUSTARD AND PARSLEY. DREDGE SHORT RIBS IN THE MIXTURE. BROWN MEAT IN OIL WITH ONION. ADD GARLIC, BEER (AND WATER IF NECESSARY TO MAKE ONE INCH OF LIQUID). COVER AND BAKE AT 300° FOR 2½ HOURS OR UNTIL MEAT IS TENDER. ADD CARROTS DURING THE LAST 20 MINUTES. REMOVE GARLIC. SERVE WITH RICE AND A SALAD.

IF IT IS SUCH A SMALL WORLD, WHY DOES IT COST SO MUCH TO RUN IT?

Chicken & Wild Rice Casserole

1	cup wild rice - cooked
½	cup chopped onion
½	cup butter
¼	cup flour
1	10 oz. can sliced mushrooms
1	cup (about) chicken broth
1½	cups light cream
3	cups diced chicken - cooked
¼	cup diced pimento
2	tbsps. snipped parsley
1½	tsps. salt
¼	tsp. pepper
½	cup slivered almonds

Cook onion in butter until tender but not brown. Remove from heat and stir in flour. Drain mushrooms, reserving liquid. Add chicken broth to mushroom liquid to measure 1½ cups. Gradually add to flour mixture. Add cream, cook and stir until thick. Add cooked wild rice, mushrooms, chicken, pimento, parsley, salt and pepper. Place in 2 quart casserole, sprinkle with almonds. Bake in 350° oven for 30 minutes. Serves 8.

When my wife has an accident in the kitchen, I get it for dinner.

JAMBALAYA

A RECIPE THAT REMINDS ME OF EVERY ROMANTIC BOOK ABOUT THE "OLD SOUTH". (SEE PICTURE, COVER).

2	CUPS DICED HAM
2	TBSPS. BUTTER
2	CHICKEN BREASTS
6	SLICES BACON, COOKED AND CRUMBLED IN LARGE PIECES
1	7 OZ. CAN BROKEN SHRIMP
1	LARGE ONION, DICE FINELY
6	STALKS CELERY, CHOPPED
3	CUPS COOKED RICE
1	28 OZ. CAN TOMATOES, WITH JUICE, CHOPPED
1	TSP. SALT
½	TSP. PEPPER
½	TSP. THYME
½	TSP. WORCESTERSHIRE SAUCE
	TABASCO TO TASTE (OPTIONAL)

IN LARGE SKILLET, SAUTÉ CHICKEN BREASTS IN BUTTER 20 MINUTES OR UNTIL COOKED. REMOVE DEBONE AND DICE DECHICKEN. SAUTÉ ONION AND CELERY UNTIL TRANSPARENT. COOK RICE ACCORDING TO PACKAGE DIRECTIONS. COMBINE ALL INGREDIENTS IN SKILLET AND HEAT THROUGH FOR 10 MINUTES. THIS FREEZES WELL; ADD WATER OR TOMATO JUICE IF IT APPEARS DRY. SERVES 6.

STONED STEW

3	LBS. STEWING BEEF, CUT UP
1/4	CUP FLOUR
1/2	TSP. SALT
1/2	TSP. SEASONED PEPPER
1/4	CUP OIL
2	LARGE ONIONS, THINLY SLICED
1	10 OZ. CAN SLICED MUSHROOMS
1	10 OZ. CAN BEEF BROTH
1	12 OZ. BOTTLE OF BEER
2	TBSPS. VINEGAR
2	TSPS. SUGAR
2	CLOVES GARLIC, MINCED
1	TSP. THYME
3	BAY LEAVES
2	TBSPS. DRIED PARSLEY

IN PLASTIC BAG COMBINE FLOUR, SALT AND PEPPER. TRIM BEEF CUBES AND SHAKE IN FLOUR MIXTURE. HEAT OIL IN SKILLET AND BROWN MEAT, TURNING OFTEN. ADD SLICED ONIONS, MUSHROOMS WITH LIQUID, BEEF BROTH, BEER, VINEGAR, SUGAR, GARLIC, THYME AND BAY LEAVES. SIMMER, COVERED, ADDING WATER IF NECESSARY, FOR 2 HOURS. ADD PARSLEY. SERVE OVER HOT BUTTERED NOODLES. SERVES 8.

SIGN IN A BANKRUPT STORE WINDOW—
"WE UNDERSOLD EVERYONE"

III "BADDIES" BUT GOODIES

CAKES AND SQUARES

COOKIES

DESSERTS

Caramel Bars

ANOTHER CHILDRENS' FAVORITE!

64	KRAFT CARAMELS (14 oz. PKG.)
1	CUP EVAPORATED MILK
2	CUPS FLOUR
2	CUPS OATMEAL
1½	CUPS BROWN SUGAR
1	TSP. SODA
1	TSP. SALT
1½	CUPS BUTTER
1	12 oz. PKG. CHOCOLATE CHIPS
½	CUP WALNUTS, CHOPPED

MELT CARAMELS WITH EVAPORATED MILK IN DOUBLE BOILER. MIX FLOUR, OATMEAL, BROWN SUGAR, SODA, SALT AND BUTTER. PRESS ½ OF MIXTURE ONTO 18" x 15" JELLY ROLL PAN OR A 10" x 15" COOKIE SHEET AND AN 8" SQUARE PAN. (BAR SHOULD BE ¾" THICK WHEN COOKED). BAKE 5 MINUTES AT 350°. SPRINKLE CHOCOLATE CHIPS AND WALNUTS OVER COOKED CRUST. SPREAD CARAMEL MIXTURE OVER THAT, AND SPRINKLE THE OTHER HALF OF THE CRUMB MIXTURE ON TOP. BAKE 15 TO 20 MINUTES AT 350°, UNTIL GOLDEN BROWN. CUT WHILE WARM.

TIME MAY BE A GREAT HEALER, BUT IT'S A LOUSY BEAUTICIAN.

Lemon Bars

Crust

1	cup flour
½	cup butter
¼	cup sugar
	pinch of salt

Custard

1	cup sugar
2	tbsps. flour
¼	tsp. baking powder
	juice of one lemon (3 tbsps.), and finely grated rind
2	beaten eggs

Crust - Blend well and press into unbuttered 9" x 9" pan. Bake at 350° for 20 minutes.

Custard - Mix well and pour over bottom layer. Bake at 350° for 25 minutes. Sprinkle with icing sugar and cut when cool.

"I read your new book. Who wrote it for you?" "Who read it to you?"

Mrs. Larson's Bars

Great favorite with children.

Crust

1	cup butter
2	cups brown sugar
2	eggs - beaten
2	tsps. vanilla
2½	cups flour
1	tsp. soda
1	tsp. salt
3	cups oatmeal

Filling

1	12 oz. pkg. chocolate chips
1	14 oz. can Eagle Brand milk
2	tbsps. butter
½	tsp. salt
½	tsp. vanilla

Crust - Cream butter and sugar. Add eggs and vanilla and mix well. Sift flour, salt and soda. Add to batter and mix. Add oatmeal and mix into a crumbly texture. Reserve ¼ of this oatmeal mixture for topping. Pat remainder into bottom of an 18" x 15" jelly roll pan or two 9" x 13" pans. (Bar should be ¾" thick when cooked.)

For filling see next page.

Continued from page 159.

FILLING - Combine ingredients in top of double boiler and heat and stir until melted. Spread filling in thin layer over crust and sprinkle top with reserved oatmeal mixture. Bake at 350° for approximately 20 minutes or until golden brown.

Recipe for a REAL sponge cake —
You borrow all the ingredients!

Fluffy Icing

Wonderful for kids cake. It makes gobs!

1	cup	white sugar
1/4	tsp.	cream of tartar
1		egg white
1/2	tsp.	vanilla
1/2	cup	BOILING water

Place all ingredients in large bowl, adding boiling water last. Beat on high with electric mixer for 10 minutes. This makes enough icing for a large angel food cake or two or three cake layers. Food colouring may be added for colour.

Fantastic Fudge Brownies

Men love them – so do children,
(and moms not on diets!).

- 1 cup butter
- 2 cups sugar
- 4 heaping tbsps. cocoa
- 4 eggs, beaten
- 1 cup flour
- 1 cup walnuts, chopped
- 1 tsp. vanilla

Icing

- 2 cups icing sugar
- 2 tbsps. butter
- 2 tbsps. cocoa
- 2 tbsps. boiling water
- 2 tsps. vanilla

Cream sugar, cocoa and butter. Add beaten eggs and vanilla. Add flour and fold in walnuts. Bake in greased 9"x13" pan at 350° for 40 to 45 minutes. Top will appear to be underdone (falls in middle) but don't overcook. Should be moist and chewy. Add icing immediately after removing from oven so it will melt into a shiny glaze.

Icing – Mix ingredients together with electric beater while brownies are cooking.

Karrot's Cake

So good for your eyesight!

1	cup sugar
3/4	cup Mazola corn oil
3	eggs
1½	cups flour
2	cups finely grated carrots (4 to 5)
½	tsp. salt
1⅓	tsps. baking soda (???!!**)
1½	tsps. cinnamon

Mix oil and sugar. Beat well. Add eggs, one at a time and beat after each. Sift dry ingredients and add to egg mixture. Beat all together until well blended. Fold in raw carrots. Bake one hour at 300° in greased 9" x 13" pan.

Icing for Karrot's Cake

8	oz. pkg. Philadelphia cream cheese
4	tbsps. butter
2½	cups icing sugar
2	tsps. vanilla

Soften cheese and butter. Beat well. Add sugar and vanilla. Beat again. Spread on cooled cake.

It is more blessed to give "then" receive

162

RHUBARB CAKE

EASY AND DELICIOUS SERVED WARM.

1½	CUPS BROWN SUGAR
½	CUP BUTTER
2	EGGS
1	CUP SOUR MILK (2 TBSPS. VINEGAR, 1 CUP MILK)
1	TSP. SODA
1	TSP. SALT
2¼	CUPS FLOUR
1	TSP. VANILLA
1½	CUPS RHUBARB, CHOPPED FINE

TOPPING:

½	CUP BROWN SUGAR
1	TSP. CINNAMON

CREAM BROWN SUGAR AND BUTTER, ADD EGGS AND BEAT WELL. ADD SOUR MILK, SODA, SALT AND FLOUR. MIX WELL AND ADD VANILLA AND RHUBARB. POUR INTO 9"×13" GREASED AND FLOURED PAN. MIX BROWN SUGAR AND CINNAMON AND SPRINKLE ON BATTER. BAKE AT 350° FOR 45 MINUTES. ADD A SCOOP OF ICE CREAM AND LISTEN TO THE ACCOLADES!

AN INTERMISSION AT A COLLEGE DANCE IS WHEN EVERYONE COMES INSIDE TO REST.

WAR CAKE

This recipe was a favorite with our mothers during the early forties when eggs were rationed. An economical and very easy spice cake.

- 1 cup raisins
- 2 cups water
- 1 tsp. soda
- 1 tbsp. lard
- 1 cup sugar
- 1 tsp. cloves
- 1 tsp. nutmeg
- 1 tbsp. cinnamon
- pinch of salt
- 1½ cups flour
- ½ cup chopped walnuts (optional)
- ½ cup coconut (optional)

Combine raisins and water in a saucepan, bring to boil and simmer for 20 minutes. Add soda and lard, let cool. Add raisin mixture to dry ingredients and mix well. Pour into greased 8" square pan and bake at 350° for 20 to 25 minutes.

The best way to get a good cup of coffee in the morning is to wake up your wife first.

Christmas Cherry Cake

A delicious and never fail moist white cake and half the work of a regular Christmas cake! Freezes well.

1	cup white sugar
1	cup butter
2	eggs, beaten
½	cup orange juice
2	cups flour
1	tsp. baking powder
12	oz. sultana raisins
8	oz. halved red glace cherries

(or use half red and half green cherries)

Cream butter and sugar. Add beaten eggs and orange juice. Sift flour and baking powder. Reserve ⅓ cup of flour mixture and toss with raisins and cherries (this will keep them from sinking to the bottom of the cake). Add flour mixture to batter and blend. Add floured raisins and cherries to dough. Bake in a large, greased, wax paper lined loaf tin at 300° for 2½ hours. Don't serve until several days old. Wrap in plastic or foil wrap and store in a sealed tin.

THE ONLY THING WORSE THAN BEING OLD AND BENT IS BEING YOUNG AND BROKE.

MISSION CRY BABIES

1	CUP SHORTENING
1	CUP SUGAR
2	EGGS
½	CUP MOLASSES
1	TBSP. VINEGAR
1	CUP STRONG COFFEE
2	TSPS. BAKING SODA
2	CUPS RAISINS
4	CUPS FLOUR
2	TSPS. CINNAMON
1	TSP. GINGER
½	TSP. SALT

POUR HOT COFFEE OVER RAISINS, ADD SODA AND LET STAND. IN LARGE BOWL MEASURE SHORTENING AND SUGAR AND BEAT UNTIL LIGHT. ADD EGGS AND BEAT UNTIL LIGHT AND PALE. BEAT IN VINEGAR AND MOLASSES. THEN ADD RAISIN MIXTURE. SIFT FLOUR, SALT AND SPICES AND ADD TO MIXTURE. DROP BY SPOONFULS ONTO GREASED COOKIE SHEET AT LEAST TWO INCHES APART. BAKE AT 375° FOR 7 TO 9 MINUTES. DO NOT OVERBAKE!

ALWAYS DO RIGHT — IT WILL GRATIFY SOME PEOPLE AND ASTONISH THE OTHERS.

Chocolate Chip Cookies

Delicious, especially right out of the oven!

1	cup butter
3/4	cup brown sugar, firmly packed
1/4	cup white sugar
1	tsp. vanilla
1 1/2	cups flour
1/2	tsp. salt
1	tsp. baking soda
1/3	cup boiling water
2	cups rolled oats
1/2	cup chopped nuts
3/4	cup chocolate chips

Beat butter until soft. Add sugars and beat until fluffy. Add vanilla. Add flour and salt and mix well. Dissolve baking soda in boiling water. Blend into mixture. Stir in the rolled oats, nuts and chocolate chips. Roll in balls and flatten with fork dipped in cold water. Bake at 350° for 10 to 12 minutes. Yields 4 to 5 dozen.

By the time a man can read women like a book, he's too old to start a library.

FRUIT & NUT SHORTBREAD

A COLOURFUL ADDITION TO YOUR CHRISTMAS BAKING.

½	LB. BUTTER
1	CUP BROWN SUGAR
1	EGG YOLK
2	CUPS FLOUR
⅔	CUP GLACE CHERRIES, HALVED
½	CUP WALNUTS, CHOPPED
	WAX PAPER

CREAM BUTTER AND SUGAR. ADD YOLK AND FLOUR. CUT IN FRUIT AND NUTS. SHAPE DOUGH INTO TWO ROLLS 2" IN DIAMETER AND ROLL IN WAX PAPER. CHILL OVERNIGHT. WHILE STILL COLD AND WAX PAPER STILL ON, TAKE A SHARP KNIFE AND CUT THIN SLICES (1/8"). SET ON GREASED COOKIE SHEETS, REMOVE WAX PAPER AND BAKE AT 375° FOR 10 MINUTES. (SLIGHTLY BROWN EDGES). NOTE: TWIST COOKIES OFF SHEET.

ANYBODY WHO CAN SWALLOW AN ASPIRIN AT A DRINKING FOUNTAIN DESERVES TO GET WELL.

HERMITS - SPICED DROPPED COOKIES

THESE FAMILY FAVORITES WERE ALWAYS INCLUDED IN OUR "CARE PACKAGES" FROM HOME. WILL KEEP FOR AGES AND ARE BETTER AFTER A FEW DAYS - IF THEY LAST THAT LONG!

3/4	CUP	BUTTER
1½	CUPS	BROWN SUGAR
2		EGGS
1	TSP.	VANILLA
2	CUPS	FLOUR
½	TSP.	BAKING POWDER
½	TSP.	BAKING SODA
½	TSP.	NUTMEG
½	TSP.	GINGER
½	TSP.	MACE
1	TSP.	CINNAMON
1	CUP	RAISINS
1	CUP	CHOPPED DATES
1	CUP	WALNUTS

CREAM BUTTER AND SUGAR. BEAT IN EGGS. ADD VANILLA. SIFT FLOUR, BAKING POWDER, BAKING SODA AND SPICES. RESERVE 1/3 CUP OF THIS DRY MIXTURE AND TOSS WITH RAISINS, DATES AND NUTS. (THIS WILL KEEP THEM FROM SINKING TO THE BOTTOM OF THE COOKIE.) ADD REMAINING FLOUR MIXTURE TO BATTER AND BLEND. THIS RECIPE IS CONTINUED ON PAGE 170.

HERMITS-SPICED DROPPED COOKIES

CONTINUED FROM PAGE 169.

ADD FLOURED RAISINS, DATES AND NUTS
TO DOUGH. DROP BY SPOONFULS ONTO GREASED
BAKING SHEETS. BAKE AT (365°) FOR 10 *(Who keeps saying that?)*
MINUTES. <u>DON'T OVERCOOK</u> — SHOULD BE
SOFT AND CHEWY. MAKES AT LEAST 5 DOZEN.

IN THE 16TH CENTURY, EXERCISING WAS
CONSIDERED SINFUL. IN THE 20TH CENTURY, SIN
IS CONSIDERED A GOOD FORM OF EXERCISE!

DIAMONDS

1   CUP BUTTER
1   CUP BROWN SUGAR
1   EGG YOLK
1   CUP FLOUR
6   MILK CHOCOLATE BARS (1 OZ. EACH)
2/3 CUP SLICED FILBERTS OR ALMONDS

CREAM BUTTER, SUGAR AND EGG YOLK. ADD
FLOUR. SPREAD DOUGH ON A GREASED PAN
15" × 10" × 1". BAKE AT 350° FOR 15 TO 20
MINUTES. REMOVE FROM OVEN AND LAY
CHOCOLATE BARS ON TOP. SPREAD WHEN
MELTED. SPRINKLE WITH NUTS. WHILE WARM,
CUT INTO 75 BARS OR DIAMONDS.

Chocolate Upside Down Cake

- 1¼ cups Cake or regular flour
- ¾ cup sugar
- 2 tsps. Baking Powder
- ¼ tsp. Salt
- ½ cup broken nuts (ouch!)
- 1 oz. square bitter chocolate
- 2 tbsps. Butter
- ½ cup Milk
- 1 tsp. Vanilla

Topping:

- 2 tbsps. Cocoa
- ½ cup brown sugar
- ½ cup white sugar
- 1 cup boiling water
- ½ pint whipping cream or ice cream

Sift flour, ¾ cup white sugar, baking powder and salt together. Melt chocolate and butter together. Mix with milk and vanilla. Stir into dry ingredients. Add nuts and blend thoroughly. Pour into a well greased layer cake pan. Now, mix cocoa, brown sugar and ½ cup white sugar. Spread over top of cake batter. Pour boiling water over all. Bake in moderate 350° oven for 1 hour. It is best served slightly warm with whipped whipping cream.

ARMENIAN ORANGE CAKE

FAST, SIMPLE AND ABSOLUTELY DELICIOUS.

2	CUPS BROWN SUGAR
2	CUPS SIFTED ALL PURPOSE FLOUR
½	CUP BUTTER
½	TSP. SALT
2	TSPS. GRATED FRESH ORANGE PEEL
½	TSP. ALLSPICE
1	TSP. BAKING SODA
1	CUP DAIRY SOUR CREAM
1	EGG SLIGHTLY BEATEN
½	CUP CHOPPED NUTS (WALNUTS, CASHEWS, ALMONDS)

COMBINE BROWN SUGAR, FLOUR, BUTTER, SALT, ORANGE PEEL AND ALLSPICE IN A MEDIUM SIZED BOWL. BLEND WITH A PASTRY BLENDER OR A FORK, UNTIL MIXTURE IS CRUMBLY AND COMPLETELY BLENDED. GREASE A 9" SQUARE PAN. (A SPRING FORM PAN IS A GOOD IDEA IF SERVING AT THE TABLE). SPOON IN HALF THE CRUMB MIXTURE. STIR SODA INTO SOUR CREAM AND MIX INTO THE REMAINING CRUMBS ALONG WITH EGG. POUR BATTER OVER CRUMBS AND SPRINKLE WITH CHOPPED NUTS. BAKE IN 350° OVEN 40 TO 45 MINUTES. SERVE WARM TOPPED WITH ORANGE WHIPPED CREAM.

SEE PAGE 173 FOR THIS TOPPING!

HE HAS MONEY TO BURN AND SHE'S A PERFECT MATCH.

Armenian Orange Cake

Orange Whipped Cream Topping.

½   pint whipping cream
2   tbsps. icing sugar
1   tsp. grated orange peel
2   tbsps. Cointreau or Grand Marnier

Whip cream until stiff. Stir in sugar, peel and liqueur. Let stand for about one hour to let flavours blend.

Fresh Strawberry Delight

One of the easiest summer desserts you'll ever find. Great for casual entertaining and children are wild about it.

    Strawberries
    Sour Cream
    Brown Sugar or
        Powdered Maple Sugar

Wash and hull strawberries. Set in large serving bowl. Add sour cream to a small bowl and brown sugar to another bowl. Using a fork, dip strawberries into sour cream and then into brown sugar. Everyone does their own — absolutely delicious!

A "GRAND CAKE"

This **LONG** recipe is not as troublesome to make as the length may suggest. It can be made the day ahead if covered and refrigerated. (Hint: use a chocolate cake mix that makes two layer cakes).

1¾	cups all purpose flour
1	tsp. baking soda
½	tsp. baking powder
1	tsp. salt
½	cup cocoa
½	cup butter
1⅔	cups granulated sugar
3	eggs
1	tsp. vanilla
1⅓	cups water
¼	cup grand marnier
6	oz. frozen concentrated orange juice — unsweeted
¾	cup granulated sugar
1	envelope gelatin (1 tbsp.)
	coarsely grated peel of 2 oranges
¼	cup grand marnier
1	pint whipping cream
¾	cup icing sugar

You'll find out how to put this together on the next page!

A "Grand Cake"

This is how you put it all together! Preheat oven to 350°. Grease two 8" round cake pans. Line with wax paper and grease again. Measure flour, baking soda, baking powder, salt and cocoa into a bowl and stir together until well blended. Cream butter in a large mixing bowl using electric beater. Gradually add sugar, beating until light and fluffy. Beat in eggs one at a time. Add vanilla. At low speed, beat in 1/3 of flour mixture, then 1/2 water, beating only until mixed after each addition. Beat in another 1/3 flour, remaining water and rest of flour.

Turn into prepared pans and bang on counter to remove air bubbles. Bake for 30 to 35 minutes or until centre of cake springs back when lightly touched. Let cakes cool 5 minutes, then turn out. Remove wax paper and cool thoroughly on racks.

An hour or two before assembling, slice each in half horizontally to make four layers. Place layers, cut side up, on waxed paper and sprinkle each with 1 tbsp. of Grand Marnier.

This recipe is continued on next page!

Memory is what tells a man his wedding anniversary was yesterday.

A "GRAND CAKE"

CONTINUED FROM PAGE 175.

FOR THE FILLING COMBINE JUICE CONCENTRATE, SUGAR AND GELATIN IN A SAUCEPAN AND COOK OVER MEDIUM HEAT, STIRRING CONSTANTLY UNTIL SUGAR AND GELATIN ARE DISSOLVED (5 MINUTES). REMOVE FROM HEAT AND STIR IN ORANGE PEEL AND 1/4 CUP GRAND MARNIER. PRESS A SHEET OF WAXED PAPER ON TO SURFACE AND REFRIGERATE FOR 20 MINUTES UNTIL IT NO LONGER FEELS WARM.

MEANWHILE, WHIP CREAM IN A LARGE BOWL UNTIL SOFT PEAKS FORM. GRADUALLY BEAT IN ICING SUGAR. THEN FOLD IN GRAND MARNIER MIXTURE.

TO ASSEMBLE, PLACE ONE LAYER OF CAKE, CUT SIDE UP, ON SERVING PLATE. SPOON 1/4 FILLING AND SPREAD. TOP WITH ANOTHER LAYER AND CONTINUE UNTIL ALL ARE USED. END WITH FILLING. REFRIGERATE IMMEDIATELY, LET SET AT LEAST 4 HOURS TO BLEND FLAVOURS.

THE BEACH IS A PLACE AT THE SEASHORE WHERE PEOPLE LIE ABOUT HOW RICH THEY ARE IN TOWN.

PICTURED ON OVERLEAF:

DESSERTS

MOCHA TORTE DESSERT
MELON IN RUM SAUCE
CHOCOLATE POTS DE CRÊME
ENGLISH TRIFLE

CHOCOLATE POUNDCAKE

3	CUPS SIFTED ALL PURPOSE FLOUR
1/2	CUP COCOA
1/2	TSP. BAKING POWDER
1/4	TSP. SALT
1	CUP BUTTER
1/2	CUP SOFT SHORTENING
3	CUPS SUGAR
5	EGGS
1 1/4	CUPS MILK
2	TBSPS. GRATED, UNSWEETENED CHOCOLATE
1	TSP. VANILLA

PREHEAT OVEN TO 350°. LIGHTLY GREASE AND FLOUR 10" TUBE PAN. SIFT FLOUR WITH COCOA, BAKING POWDER AND SALT. SET ASIDE. IN LARGE BOWL BEAT BUTTER, SHORTENING AND SUGAR FOR 5 MINUTES. ADD EGGS ONE AT A TIME, BEATING WELL AFTER EACH ADDITION. WITH MIXER AT LOW SPEED, BEAT IN FLOUR MIXTURE IN FOUR ADDITIONS, ALTERNATING WITH THE MILK IN THREE ADDITIONS, ENDING WITH THE FLOUR. ADD GRATED CHOCOLATE AND VANILLA. TURN BATTER INTO PREPARED PAN. BAKE 1 HOUR AND 15 TO 20 MINUTES OR TILL TESTER INSERTED IN CENTRE COMES OUT CLEAN. LET COOL ON WIRE RACK FOR 10 MINUTES, TURN OUT AND LET COOL COMPLETELY. IF DESIRED, SERVE WITH WHIPPED CREAM AND SHAVED CHOCOLATE.

Cardinal's Lime Special

These meringues may be made ahead and stored in a cool dry place.

      5   eggs
      1/4 tsp. cream of tartar
      1   cup sugar
      1/4 tsp. pistachio flavouring
      4   tbsps. lime juice
      2   tsps. grated lime rind
      1/2 cup sugar
      1   cup whipping cream

Separate 4 of the eggs and beat whites until stiff. Add cream of tartar. Add sugar a tablespoon at a time continuing to beat. Add pistachio flavouring and beat mixture for 20 minutes in all.

Use two well greased cookie sheets. With 8" pie plate draw circles on cookie sheets. Spread mixture on circles, building up sides with spoon. Bake at 275° for 20 minutes. Turn oven up to 300° and bake 40 minutes longer. Cool completely.

Now, beat egg yolks and fifth egg until thick. Beat in lime juice, rind and sugar. Cook in double boiler until thick, stirring occasionally. Cool. Loosen crusts.

This recipe continued page 179.

CARDINAL'S LIME SPECIAL

CONTINUED FROM PAGE 178.

WHIP CREAM AND SPREAD ¼ OVER EACH CRUST, THEN ½ OF THE FILLING ON EACH. TOP WITH REMAINING WHIPPED CREAM. PLACE CRUSTS, ONE ON TOP OF THE OTHER, RIGHT SIDE UP. CHILL 24 HOURS. SERVES 6 TO 8. (LEMON JUICE AND RIND MAY BE SUBSTITUTED FOR LIME BUT USE ALMOND FLAVOURING FOR THE PISTACHIO FLAVOURING IN THE MERINGUES.)

PECAN PIE

3	EGGS
1	CUP WHITE SYRUP (KARO)
⅛	TSP. SALT
1	CUP SUGAR
1	TSP. VANILLA
1	CUP WHOLE PECANS
1	9" PIE SHELL (UNCOOKED)

BEAT EGGS. ADD SYRUP, SALT, SUGAR AND VANILLA. BEAT UNTIL WELL MIXED. ADD PECANS. POUR INTO PIE SHELL. BAKE AT 450° FOR 10 MINUTES. REDUCE TO 350° AND BAKE FOR A FURTHER 30 MINUTES. SERVE WITH WHIPPED CREAM OR ICE CREAM, IF DESIRED. IF YOU HAVE A FROZEN PIE SHELL ON HAND, THIS PIE CAN BE WHIPPED UP IN MINUTES. TERRIFIC FOR THOSE UNEXPECTED GUESTS – AND YOU ALWAYS THOUGHT IT WAS SO DIFFICULT! SERVES 6 TO 8.

CHOCOLATE MUD PIE

1	8½ oz. package chocolate wafers
½	cup butter
1½	pts. coffee ice cream, softened
⅓	cup cocoa
3	tbsps. butter
⅔	cup sugar & 2 tbsps. sugar
1⅓	cups whipping cream
2	tsps. vanilla extract
2	squares semisweet chocolate,
	-for garnish

EARLY IN DAY:

Crush chocolate wafers into fine crumbs. In small saucepan over low heat, melt ½ cup butter. In 9" pie plate combine crumbs and butter and press mixture to bottom and side of plate. Bake at 375° for 10 mins. Cool crust completely on wire rack. Carefully spread coffee ice cream into crust; freeze until firm, about 1½ hours.

In large saucepan over medium heat, cook cocoa, ⅔ cup sugar, ⅓ cup of whipping cream and 3 tbsps. butter until mixture is smooth and boils. Remove from heat and stir in 1 tsp. vanilla. Cool mixture slightly then pour over coffee ice cream. Return pie to freezer, freezing at least one hour.

To serve, see page 181.

Chocolate Mud Pie

TO SERVE: IN SMALL BOWL AND WITH MIXER AT MEDIUM SPEED, BEAT REMAINING WHIPPING CREAM WITH 2 TBSP. SUGAR AND 1 TSP. VANILLA UNTIL SOFT PEAKS FORM. SPREAD WHIPPED CREAM OVER PIE. GARNISH WITH CHOCOLATE CURLS. MAKES 10 SERVINGS.

Chocolate Mocha Mousse

1	7 OZ. PKG. CHOCOLATE WAFERS
1/4	CUP MELTED BUTTER
1	CUP BOILING WATER
4	TSPS. INSTANT COFFEE
1	11 OZ. PKG. MARSHMALLOWS
1/2	PT. WHIPPING CREAM

MELT MARSHMALLOWS IN THE TOP OF A DOUBLE BOILER. ADD INSTANT COFFEE TO BOILING WATER AND STIR INTO MARSHMALLOWS. CHILL AT LEAST ONE HOUR. RESERVE 14 CHOCOLATE WAFERS AND CRUSH REST OF PACKAGE. SET ASIDE 1 TBSP. CRUSHED WAFERS FOR TOPPING. ADD BUTTER TO REMAINING WAFER CRUMBS AND PRESS INTO BOTTOM OF SPRING FORM PAN. PLACE THE 14 WAFERS AROUND EDGE OF PAN. WHIP CREAM. REMOVE COFFEE MIXTURE FROM FRIG AND WHIP. FOLD CREAM AND COFFEE MIXTURE TOGETHER AND POUR INTO PAN. ADD TOPPING AND CHILL. SERVES 6.

Chocolate Cheese Torte

This is very rich, very expensive but very, very good!

1⅓	cups graham wafer cracker crumbs
3	tbsps. sugar
3	tbsps. unsweetened cocoa powder
⅓	cup butter, melted
4	pkgs. (3 oz. size) cream cheese
¾	cup sugar
2	eggs
1	tbsp. coffee flavoured liqueur or rum
1	tsp. vanilla
1	8 oz. carton sour cream
1	sq. unsweetened chocolate, grated
1½	tsp. instant coffee powder
2	tbsps. boiling water
4	sq. semi-sweet chocolate
4	eggs, separated
⅓	cup sugar
1	tbsp. coffee flavoured liqueur or rum
½	tsp. vanilla
½	cup whipping cream, whipped

This recipe is continued on next page!

My wife made U.F.O.s yesterday- unidentified FRYING objects.

Chocolate Cheese Torte

Here's how to put it together...
Preheat oven to 350°. Blend crumbs, sugar, cocoa and butter together until well blended. Press firmly onto bottom and side of 9" spring form pan. Bake for 10 minutes. Cool while preparing filling.

Beat cream cheese in a large bowl with electric beater at high speed until light and fluffy. Gradually beat in sugar. Add 2 eggs, one at a time, beating well after each addition. Add liqueur and vanilla. Turn into baked crust. Bake at 350° for 30 minutes. Cool for 10 minutes on wire rack.

Gently spread sour cream over baked layer. Sprinkle with grated chocolate. Refrigerate.

Dissolve coffee in boiling water in double boiler over hot - not boiling - water. Add chocolate. Stir until melted and blended.

Beat the 4 egg yolks until thick. Gradually beat in sugar and a small amount of chocolate mixture. Beat well. Continue adding small amounts of chocolate mixture to egg mixture, until all has been used. Add liqueur and vanilla.

Beat egg whites until fluffy. Gently fold into chocolate mixture. Spread over cooled baked layer. Refrigerate until firm. When ready to serve loosen side of pan, remove. Place cake on serving plate. Decorate with whipped cream. Serves 12.

ENGLISH TRIFLE
(SEE PICTURE).

1	SPONGE CAKE, STALE
20	oz. PACKAGE FROZEN RASPBERRIES OR STRAWBERRIES
½	CUP MEDIUM SHERRY
1	CUP WHIPPED CREAM
	TOASTED ALMONDS
	MARASCHINO CHERRIES
	SHERRY CUSTARD - SEE PAGE 185.

Cut sponge cake into slices and arrange in a layer in the bottom of a large glass serving bowl. Spoon a layer of semi-thawed fruit over cake. Spoon a layer of sherry custard over fruit and repeat layers finishing with a layer of custard. Pour ¼ cup sherry over all and refrigerate 2 hours. Pour remaining sherry over all - inserting a silver knife to the bottom in several places so the sherry will soak through. Allow to mellow in frig for at least 24 hours. Just before serving, whip cream and spread over the top. Decorate with almonds and cherries.

SPEAK WELL OF YOUR ENEMIES —
REMEMBER — YOU MADE THEM!

SHERRY CUSTARD

For English Trifle:

- 4 egg yolks
- ½ cup granulated sugar
- pinch of salt
- 1 tbsp. flour
- ½ to 1 cup medium sherry
- 4 egg whites, beaten stiff

In top part of double boiler, combine egg yolks, sugar, salt, flour and sherry. Cook over hot water and stir constantly until mixture thickens — about 7 minutes. Remove from heat immediately and fold in stiffly beaten egg whites. This is now ready to be added to English trifle recipe as described on page 184.

Food prices are changing our whole way of life. Now parents tell their children, "Eat your dessert or you won't get your meat."

GRASSHOPPER CAKE

A VERY SPECIAL DESSERT. THE CAKE CAN BE MADE AHEAD AND FROZEN. ADD FILLING THE DAY OF SERVING. SERVES 10 TO 12.

CAKE

2	EGG WHITES
1/2	CUP SUGAR
1 3/4	CUPS SIFTED SWANSDOWN CAKE FLOUR
1	CUP SUGAR
3/4	TSP. BAKING SODA
1	TSP. SALT
1/3	CUP OIL
1	CUP BUTTERMILK (BUY A BOX OF BUTTERMILK AND AVOID LEFTOVERS) OR SOUR MILK (2 TBSPS. VINEGAR TO 1 CUP MILK)
2	EGG YOLKS
2	SQUARES UNSWEETENED CHOCOLATE, MELTED

FILLING

1	ENVELOPE GELATIN
1/4	CUP COLD WATER
1/3	CUP GREEN CREME DE MENTHE LIQUEUR
1/3	CUP WHITE CREME DE CACAO LIQUEUR
1	PINT (2 CTNS.) WHIPPING CREAM

THIS RECIPE IS CONTINUED ON NEXT PAGE!

GRASSHOPPER CAKE

HERE'S WHAT YOU DO.....

CAKE

PREHEAT OVEN TO 350°. GREASE AND FLOUR TWO 8" ROUND PANS (AT LEAST 1½" DEEP). BEAT EGG WHITES UNTIL FOAMY. ADD ½ CUP SUGAR, 1 TBSP. AT A TIME, BEATING WELL AFTER EACH ADDITION. BEAT UNTIL STIFF AND GLOSSY. SIFT FLOUR, 1 CUP SUGAR, SODA AND SALT INTO LARGE MIXING BOWL. ADD OIL, HALF OF THE BUTTER-MILK (½ CUP) AND BEAT ONE MINUTE AT MEDIUM SPEED. ADD REMAINING BUTTERMILK (½ CUP), EGG YOLKS AND MELTED CHOCOLATE. BEAT ONE MINUTE MORE. FOLD IN EGG WHITES. BAKE 40 TO 45 MINUTES, OR UNTIL SPONGY. DON'T WORRY IF THE CAKE SEEMS DRY—ALL THAT FILLING WILL SOLVE EVERYTHING.

FILLING

ADD GELATIN TO COLD WATER AND SOAK 5 MINUTES. HEAT (BUT DO NOT BOIL) THE LIQUEURS. ADD GELATIN AND STIR TO DISSOLVE. COOL THOROUGHLY! BEAT THE WHIPPING CREAM UNTIL STIFF AND FOLD LIQUEUR MIXTURE INTO CREAM. CHILL FOR 15 MINUTES.

CUT EACH CAKE LAYER IN TWO (ANY ACCIDENTS ARE EASILY HIDDEN IN THE FILLING!). SPREAD FILLING BETWEEN ALL LAYERS AND COVER TOP AND SIDES. CHILL UNTIL SERVING.

CHEESECAKE CUPCAKES

24	PAPER MUFFIN CUPS
1	PKG. VANILLA WAFERS
1	CUP SUGAR
3	8OZ. PKGS. CREAM CHEESE, SOFTENED
4	EGGS
2	TSPS. LEMON JUICE
	CHERRY PIE FILLING,
	(OR BLUEBERRY OR RASPBERRY)

PREHEAT OVEN TO 350° MIX SUGAR, CHEESE, EGGS AND LEMON JUICE UNTIL SMOOTH. LINE CUPCAKE PANS WITH PAPERS. PLACE ONE VANILLA WAFER IN THE BOTTOM OF EACH. SPOON CHEESE MIXTURE OVER WAFERS TO FILL CUPS 3/4 FULL. BAKE IN PREHEATED OVEN FOR 18 TO 20 MINUTES. COOL. CUPCAKES WILL SINK IN THE MIDDLE WHILE COOLING. SPOON PIE FILLING ON EACH CUPCAKE, AND REFRIGERATE AT LEAST ONE HOUR. THESE MAY BE TOPPED WITH A WHIPPED TOPPING IF DESIRED. SERVES 24.

EVERY YEAR IT TAKES LESS TIME TO FLY ACROSS THE OCEAN, AND LONGER TO DRIVE TO WORK.

Apricot Smooch

A beautifully light, refreshing dessert to serve at bridge or after a heavy meal. It can also be made ahead and frozen.

- ½ cup crushed vanilla wafers
- ½ cup soft butter
- ½ cup icing sugar
- 1 egg
- 1 cup whipping cream, whipped
- ½ tsp. almond extract or apricot liqueur
- ¼ tsp. vanilla
- 3 small tins junior strained apricots (baby food)

Chopped nuts to cover top.

Grease 8" x 8" pan. Sprinkle with half the crumbs. Beat butter and sugar together. Add egg and flavourings. Beat well. Spread over crumbs with the back of a wet spoon. Cover with apricots. Cover all with whipped cream and sprinkle with remaining crumbs and chopped nuts. Freeze. Remove from freezer one hour before serving. Serves 6 to 8.

Chocolate Roll

5   EGGS

1/2   TSP. CREAM OF TARTAR

1   CUP SUGAR

1/4   CUP FLOUR

3   TBSPS. COCOA

1   TSP. VANILLA

1   PINT WHIPPING CREAM, WHIPPED

SEPARATE EGGS. BEAT WHITES WITH THE CREAM OF TARTAR UNTIL STIFF. GRADUALLY BEAT IN 1/2 CUP OF SUGAR. SIFT REMAINING SUGAR, COCOA AND FLOUR. BEAT YOLKS UNTIL THICK. FOLD FLOUR MIXTURE INTO YOLKS. ADD VANILLA – (THIS WILL BE VERY STIFF). CAREFULLY FOLD YOLK MIXTURE INTO BEATEN WHITES.

PREHEAT OVEN TO 325°. LINE COOKIE SHEET (15 1/2" x 10 1/2") WITH WAX PAPER. GREASE AND FLOUR. SPREAD BATTER EVENLY ON PAN. BAKE FOR 20 MINUTES. COOL 5 MINUTES AND TURN ONTO TOWEL SPRINKLED WITH ICING SUGAR. PEEL OFF WAX PAPER AND ROLL CAKE WITH TOWEL. COOL. WHIP CREAM AND SPREAD ON UNROLLED CAKE. ROLL AGAIN.

SERVE WITH BUTTER OR FUDGE SAUCE, PAGE 191. FOR VARIATION, ADD 2 TBSPS. RUM OR YOUR FAVORITE LIQUEUR TO THE WHIPPED CREAM. SERVES 8.

FOAMY BUTTER SAUCE

½ CUP BUTTER
1 EGG
1 CUP ICING SUGAR

COMBINE ALL INGREDIENTS IN TOP OF
DOUBLE BOILER. COOK, STIRRING UNTIL
IT FORMS A SMOOTH SAUCE.

SERVE WARM OVER CHOCOLATE ROLL.

IT'S AN ILL WIND THAT BLOWS THE
MINUTE YOU LEAVE THE BEAUTY PARLOR.

FUDGE SAUCE

1 TBSP. BUTTER
1 SQUARE UNSWEETENED
    CHOCOLATE (1 OZ.)
⅓ CUP BOILING WATER
1 CUP SUGAR
2 TBSPS. CORN SYRUP
½ TSP. VANILLA

MELT BUTTER AND CHOCOLATE IN
MEDIUM SAUCEPAN. ADD BOILING WATER.
BRING MIXTURE TO BOIL. ADD SUGAR
AND SYRUP. BOIL, STIRRING, FOR 5 MINS.
ADD VANILLA AND STIR.

SERVE JUST WARM OVER CHOCOLATE ROLL.

LEMON PUDDING

An old family favorite! The top turns to cake and the bottom turns to sauce. Serve warm with whipped cream.

- 2 tbsps. flour
- 1 cup sugar
- 2 tbsps. butter
- 2 eggs
- 1 cup milk
- Juice and grated rind (1 tbsp.) of 1 lemon

Mix flour and sugar in a shallow casserole dish. Cream butter into mixture. Separate eggs. Beat yolks and milk together. Add to mixture in casserole dish and beat until smooth. Add lemon juice and rind. Beat egg whites until stiff. Fold into mixture. Set casserole in dish of hot water. Bake 35 to 40 minutes at 350°. Brown lightly under broiler. Serves 5.

I love playing the violin, especially when I am depressed; it helps me keep my chin up.

CHOCOLATE POTS DE CRÊME

SHORT-CUT METHOD FOR THAT FAMOUS
DESSERT. (SEE PICTURE).

1   6 OZ. PKG. SEMI-SWEET CHOCOLATE CHIPS

2   TBSPS. SUGAR

     PINCH OF SALT

1   EGG

1   TSP. VANILLA

1½ TO 2 TSPS. DARK RUM OR . . . .

          1 TSP. POWDERED INSTANT COFFEE

3/4   CUP MILK

      WHIPPED CREAM, FOR TOPPING

COMBINE CHOCOLATE, SUGAR, SALT, EGG,
VANILLA AND RUM IN BLENDER. HEAT MILK JUST
TO BOILING. POUR OVER OTHER INGREDIENTS.
COVER AND BLEND 1 MINUTE. POUR IMMEDIATELY
INTO CHOCOLATE POTS OR RAMEKINS. CHILL AT
LEAST 1 HOUR. SERVE WITH WHIPPED CREAM.
SERVES 4.

ON A TENNIS PLAYERS T-SHIRT:
"NEVER FALL IN LOVE WITH A TENNIS
PLAYER. TO HIM, LOVE MEANS NOTHING!"

Danish Rum Soufflé

AN ALL TIME FAVOURITE - PARTICULARLY WITH THE MEN. MAKE IT THE DAY BEFORE!

4	EGG YOLKS
1/2	CUP SUGAR
1/4	CUP DARK RUM
1	ENVELOPE (1 TBSP.) PLAIN GELATIN
1/4	CUP COLD WATER
1/2	PINT WHIPPING CREAM
4	EGG WHITES
1/2	CUP SUGAR
1/2	PINT WHIPPING CREAM, FOR TOPPING
	HERSHEY'S SEMI-SWEET CHOCOLATE BAR
	- ROOM TEMPERATURE

BEAT EGG YOLKS AND 1/2 CUP SUGAR IN A LARGE BOWL UNTIL LEMON COLOURED. ADD RUM AND BEAT. DISSOLVE GELATIN IN COLD WATER AND SET IN SLIGHTLY LARGER BOWL OF HOT WATER TO KEEP GELATIN MIXTURE LIQUID. BEAT CREAM UNTIL STIFF. BEAT EGG WHITES UNTIL STIFF AND GRADUALLY ADD 1/2 CUP SUGAR. ADD GELATIN MIXTURE TO YOLK MIXTURE. FOLD WHIPPED CREAM INTO YOLK MIXTURE. FINALLY, FOLD IN EGG WHITES. POUR INTO CRYSTAL BOWL OR INDIVIDUAL SHERBET DISHES. CHILL 4 TO 6 HOURS OR OVERNIGHT. JUST BEFORE SERVING, TOP WITH WHIPPED CREAM AND POTATO PEELER CURLS OF CHOCOLATE. SERVES 8.

DATE TORTE

Very rich and very bad for you! We love it!

1 lb. pkg. pitted dates
1 cup walnuts
1 tsp. baking powder
1 heaping tbsp. flour
3 eggs
1 tsp. vanilla
1 cup sugar

Grind together dates and walnuts. Use food processor or meatgrinder. Beat egg yolks and whites separately. Add beaten yolks to date-walnut mixture and blend. Mix in baking powder, flour, sugar and vanilla. Fold in the beaten egg whites. Bake in greased 8"x8" pan for approximately 40 minutes at 365° (can you believe that?!). Serve warm in squares topped with whipped cream or ice cream.

Conversation overheard at a boy's camp: "We're going home tomorrow. Guess I better rumple my pyjamas and squeeze out half my toothpaste."

DUTCH APPLE CAKE

2	CUPS FLOUR
3	TSPS. BAKING POWDER
1/2	TSP. SALT
3	TBSPS. SUGAR
1/4	CUP BUTTER
1	EGG
3/4	CUP MILK
2 OR 3	CUPS SLICED APPLES
1/2	CUP SUGAR, MIXED WITH...
1	TSP. CINNAMON

SIFT FIRST FOUR INGREDIENTS TOGETHER. WORK IN THE BUTTER. BEAT EGG AND MILK AND STIR INTO DRY INGREDIENTS. SPREAD THE DOUGH IN SHALLOW GREASED 8" x 8" PAN. COVER WITH ROWS OF APPLES, PRESSING THE SHARP EDGES OF THE PIECES OF APPLES INTO DOUGH. SPRINKLE WITH SUGAR AND CINNAMON MIXTURE. BAKE 30 MINUTES AT 350°. SERVE WARM WITH WHIPPED CREAM OR ICE CREAM.

MAN IN A BUTCHER SHOP:
"I WOULDN'T PAY $2.00 FOR A POUND OF RIBS IF THEY WERE ATTACHED TO RAQUEL WELCH!"

LINCOLN CENTRE DELICATESSEN
CHOCOLATE ICE BOX PIE

1	BAKED 8" PIE SHELL
3/4	CUP ICING SUGAR
1/4	CUP BUTTER
1/4	CUP (2 SQUARES) SEMI-SWEET CHOCOLATE
1/2	TSP. VANILLA
3	EGGS
1/2	PINT WHIPPING CREAM.
	CHOCOLATE SHAVINGS (SEMI-SWEET
	HERSHEY BAR IS BEST)

CREAM SUGAR AND BUTTER. MELT CHOCOLATE IN DOUBLE BOILER AND BEAT INTO MIXTURE USING ELECTRIC BEATER. ADD VANILLA. ADD EGGS, ONE AT A TIME, BEATING EACH EGG THOROUGHLY AT HIGH SPEED (2 TO 3 MINUTES EACH EGG). POUR MIXTURE INTO BAKED <u>COOLED</u> PIE SHELL. FREEZE UNTIL SERVING TIME.

TOP WITH WHIPPED CREAM AND GARNISH WITH CHOCOLATE CURLS. (A SEMI-SWEET HERSHEY BAR AT ROOM TEMPERATURE WORKS BEST.) SERVES 6.

MOHAMMED'S WIVES: PROPHET SHARES.

MELON IN RUM SAUCE

THIS LIGHT SUMMER DESSERT IS MOST APPETIZING SERVED IN A LARGE GLASS BOWL. (SEE PICTURE).

- 1 CANTALOUPE
- 1 HONEY DEW MELON
- 1/4 OF A SMALL WATERMELON
- 1 CUP FRESH OR FROZEN BLUEBERRIES
  (DRAIN WELL IF FROZEN)

CUT MELON INTO BALLS AND ADD BERRIES—CHILL.

SAUCE:

- 2/3 CUP SUGAR
- 1/3 CUP WATER
- 1 TSP. LIME RIND
- 6 TBSPS. LIME JUICE
- 1/2 CUP LIGHT RUM

MIX SUGAR WITH WATER IN SAUCEPAN—BRING TO BOIL, THEN REDUCE HEAT AND SIMMER FOR 5 MINUTES. ADD LIME RIND AND LET COOL TO ROOM TEMPERATURE. STIR IN LIME JUICE AND RUM. POUR OVER FRUIT AND CHILL SEVERAL HOURS. SERVES 6 TO 8.

CUCUMBER PATCH: DILLIES OF THE FIELD.

Mocha Torte Dessert

Delicious and so lovely to look at! A great change for that 40th birthday! (See picture).

> 1   Chocolate Cake Mix

Mocha Cream Filling:

½	cup chocolate semi-sweet chipits
2	tbsps. hot water
2	tsps. instant coffee powder
¼	cup granulated sugar
½	pint (1¼ cup) whipping cream

Prepare cake according to package instructions. Bake in 2-8" round cake pans which have been greased and lined with circles of waxed paper. Bake and cool, then turn out on wire racks. With a knife, split each layer into two. Prepare mocha cream by combining chipits, water, coffee powder and sugar in a small, heavy saucepan. Heat, stirring until smooth, and cool. Whip cream until it starts to thicken; add chocolate mixture and whip until stiff. Spread between layers and on top of torte. Chill at least one hour. Decorate with shaved chocolate. Serves 10 to 12.

Tia Maria Cake

- 1   LARGE ANGEL FOOD CAKE
- ½   CUP TIA MARIA LIQUEUR
- 2   TBSPS. WHIPPING CREAM
- 2   CUPS WHIPPING CREAM
- 2   TBSPS. TIA MARIA LIQUEUR
- 2   TBSPS. ICING SUGAR
- 6   ALMOND ROCA CHOCOLATE BARS

CUT CAKE INTO TWO LAYERS. PLACE EACH ON A PLATE. COMBINE ½ CUP TIA MARIA AND 2 TBSPS. CREAM. PRICK CAKE ALL OVER WITH SKEWER — BOTH LAYERS. DRIZZLE TIA MIXTURE OVER ALL PARTS OF EACH LAYER; BOTTOM AND TOP. COVER WITH SARAN WRAP AND CHILL SEVERAL HOURS. TWO HOURS BEFORE SERVING, WHIP TWO CUPS OF CREAM AND FOLD IN 2 TBSPS. TIA MARIA AND THE ICING SUGAR. ICE CAKE, INCLUDING LAYERS. CRUSH ALMOND ROCA AND TOSS OVER TOP AND SIDES OF CAKE. CHILL UNTIL SERVING TIME. SERVES 10 TO 12.

ONCE WOMEN WORE BATHING SUITS DOWN TO THEIR ANKLES, THEN DOWN TO THEIR KNEES, THEN DOWN TO THEIR HIPS. THIS YEAR NO ONE IS EVEN SURE THAT THEY'LL WEAR THEM DOWN TO THE BEACH!

INDEX
BRUNCH 'N LUNCH

TOASTED TOMATO
     CHEESIES –   34

THE MAYOR'S WIFE'S
     BLUE PLUM RELISH– 38

JAM AND RELISH
CHRISTMAS MARMALADE– 37

BEST BUFFETS

APPETIZERS

ARTICHOKE NIBBLERS– 41
CRAB MOUSSE– 42
CURRIED SCALLOPS– 44
CURRIED SEAFOOD
     COCKTAIL PUFFS– 43
CURRY DIP FOR
     VEGETABLE PLATTER–45
HAM AND CHEESE BALL– 49
HA' PENNIES–
     GOD BLESS YOU– 46
HOT CHEESE SPREAD– 45
JOHNNY'S MOMMY'S PATÉ– 47
LOBSTER DIP– 48
MAD MADELEINE'S
     CHEESE PUFFS– 50
PURK'S POO-POO'S– 53
RUMAKI– 51
RUTH'S CHOKES– 52

SESAME CHEESE– 54
SHRIMP DIP– 54
SMOKED SALMON
     HORS D'OEUVRE– 53
CRUNCHY SHRIMP– 49

NUTS

CARAMELLED WALNUTS–55
CRAZY CRUNCH– 58
NOVEL NUTS– 56
SOYA ALMONDS– 55
SPICED CASHEWS
     OR PECANS– 57
TOM'S TRAIL MIX– 57

SALADS

ARMENIAN SPINACH
     SALAD– 70

SUPPER CASSEROLES

"Baddies" but Goodies

A GREAT GIFT IDEA

PLEASE SEND ME:

_____ COPIES OF "THE BEST OF BRIDGE" AT $19.95 EACH.

_____ COPIES OF "ENJOY" AT $19.95 EACH.

_____ COPIES OF "WINNERS" AT $19.95 EACH.

_____ COPIES OF "GRAND SLAM" AT $19.95 EACH.

_____ COPIES OF "ACES" AT $19.95 EACH.

_____ COPIES OF "THAT'S TRUMP" AT $19.95 EACH.

_____ PLUS $4.00 MAILING (EACH ADDRESS)

_____ SUBTOTAL

_____ PLUS GST (SUBTOTAL X .07) CANADA ONLY

$ _____ TOTAL (U.S. ORDERS - PLEASE PAY IN U.S. FUNDS)

METHOD OF PAYMENT:

24-HOUR TOLL-FREE NUMBER: 1-800-883-4674

☐ ENCLOSED IS MY CHEQUE OR MONEY ORDER PAYABLE TO:

THE BEST OF BRIDGE PUBLISHING LTD.
6037-6TH STREET S.E., CALGARY, ALBERTA, CANADA T2H 1L8

CHARGE TO: ☐ VISA   ☐ MASTERCARD

| | | | | | | | | | | | | | | | | | | | | | | | |
ACCOUNT NUMBER   EXP. DATE

SIGNATURE: _____

TELEPHONE: _____
                (IN CASE WE HAVE A QUESTION ABOUT YOUR ORDER)

SOLD TO:

NAME: _____

ADDRESS: _____

CITY: _____

PROV./STATE _____ POSTAL/ZIP CODE _____

SHIP TO:

NAME: _____

ADDRESS: _____

CITY: _____

PROV./STATE _____ POSTAL/ZIP CODE _____